E

EASTBOURNE AT WAR
Portrait of a Front Line Town

Courage personified in nine smiling faces and the two 250kg (550lb) bombs these men have just dug out and defused. No glamour job, theirs, just hard, tedious work, sheer guts and great skill. The price of failure was life itself.

George Humphrey

This book is dedicated to all those modestly and doggedly gallant Eastbournians who stayed behind and stuck it out.

A little choild may lead us but we wun't be druv!
Old and unofficial motto of Sussex folk.

First published in 1998 by S. B. Publications,
c/o 19 Grove Road, Seaford, East Sussex BN25 1TP

© 1998 George H Humphrey

ISBN 1 85770 158 5

Designed and typeset by JEM Lewes
Printed by Island Press, 3 Cradle Hill Industrial Estate,
Seaford, East Sussex BN25 3JE
Telephone: 01323 490222

CONTENTS

Front cover picture: *The crew of a 40mm Bofors anti-aircraft gun drill on the flat roof of the Pier Pavilion (now the Blue Room). Anti-aircraft defences were conspicuous by their absence for much of the period of bombing.*
Back cover picture: *Bombed out of their home in Willoughby Crescent, Jack and Gabi Hutchinson still manage a smile as they salvage their belongings on a handcart.*

ACKNOWLEDGEMENTS

I would like to record here my heartfelt thanks to the Eastbourne Editor of Beckett Newspapers for permission to reproduce the photographs in this publication, also the innumerable people who, over the past fifty years, have so willingly assisted or tolerated my research efforts – it would be impossible to name them all.

CREDITS

Without the efforts of four men in particular this and earlier publications on the same theme would have been totally devoid of illustration. Wilf Bignell, staff photographer to TR Beckett Ltd, (proprietor of the *Eastbourne Gazette* and *Herald*), Harry Deal, freelance photographer who supplied the pictures for both the *Eastbourne Chronicle* and *Courier*; John Wills and Roy Hudson, both freelances, were ever-present whenever and wherever the bombs fell. They worked tirelessly and bravely to record for posterity the images presented by the town in its ordeal. It is to be regretted that the vast majority of their original negatives have, through the carelessness and indifference of others, been lost to us. We owe them more than can be repaid.

BIBLIOGRAPHY

Front Line Eastbourne, TS Palmer, TR Beckett.
Eastbourne 1939 to 1945, WS Hardy, Strange the Printer.
Wartime Eastbourne, George Humphrey, Beckett Features.

INTRODUCTION

G ENERALLY, we tend to think of history as being only of the past and for-
get that the present is history in the making. I was a volunteer assisting
with the reception of evacuees from London on September 3, 1939 when, at
11am we were at war with Germany. Within seconds the air raid sirens sounded a general alert and, to put it mildly, my feelings were mixed, However, one
thing was borne in on me – I was actually living through a moment of history.

The thought took root and I began to gather news items and pictures of
the war as it affected Eastbourne and, when the town was so heavily bombed,
built up a considerable store of information with the expectation that it would
prove useful to the newspapers I worked for when the war was finally over.

In September 1942 I was taken into the RAF and in my absence all my
carefully gleaned and stored files were discarded by others.

After the war, bomb disposal teams called to the town to investigate reports
of unexploded bombs (UXBs) took to dropping in at T R Beckett's (publisher
of the local newspapers) in the hope of finding clues to likely locations. And so
my researches began anew with the intention of helping them – the rest is a
by-product of that effort.

Why was Eastbourne deliberately bombed? Primarily because it was a key
feature in the German invasion plans (see page 7) but this held good for only
a few days in September 1940 After that, with one or two exceptions, the
bombing took place because the Luftwaffe aircrews who made the trip across
the Channel were mostly trainees who found Beachy Head easy to locate.
Once found, Eastbourne was conveniently to hand; once Eastbourne was
found, the protruding pier made a useful point of reference. It was as simple
as that, according to ex-Luftwaffe sources.

Raiders aborting raids on London played little part in the attacks, generally
simply unloading their bombs hereabouts at night because they were making
Beachy Head their point of reference for departure from British airspace.
Our real ordeal came in daylight and it was deliberate, not the 'wides, over-
throws and leg byes' from London raids. People died, were injured, bereaved
– generally without adequate warning. This production is a brief record of
their ordeal, bravery, fortitude and astonishing good humour in adversity.

George Humphrey
Eastbourne 1998

OPERATION SEA LION
The German invasion plan

MANY people today know little or nothing of the German proposal to invade this country in the summer/early autumn of 1940, and those who are aware of the plan generally tend to credit the Germans with superman status and assume that if the invasion had been launched, Britain would have been defeated and subjugated . . . and there lies the rub – that little word 'if'.

The fact of the matter is that despite Hitler's bombast and military posturing, the Germans were never in a position to launch such an attack with any hope of success – unless we agreed to surrender terms first.

The part played by the Royal Air Force in defeating this plan is largely confined to reference to the Battle of Britain when our fighter planes effectively knocked the fight out of the Luftwaffe, but the real causes of the defeat of Sea Lion are more complex.

In the first place, as soon as France capitulated, the German army was too busy to entertain thoughts of an invasion of Britain. In the second place, the German navy had suffered severe losses during the campaign against Norway (twenty nine assorted warships and U-boats were sunk or put out of commission) and was in no position to provide adequate protection for an invasion fleet, even if one could be found. Germany had no dedicated assault vessels other than those used for river crossings during land battles.

Thirdly, after Hitler realised that we had no intention of rolling over and playing dead, his own anger and ego had him order an invasion to be prepared by mid-August, 1940, but still there were no transport vessels available, so the German navy had recourse to summon coastal steamships, river and canal barges and lighters, tugs and motor launches etc. This never happened in sufficient numbers and so the invasion date was put back time and again.

Fourth, the German army, astonishingly naive about naval matters, demanded an assault on the broadest possible front – Lyme Bay in the west to Pegwell Bay in the east – and, unbelievably, insisted on a simultaneous touch-down time on all the assault beaches, completely ignoring the fact that tidal conditions precluded any such thing. The navy pointed out that not only was the latter demand quite impossible, but that it would never be able to transport and protect a force of such size against any counter moves by the Royal Navy.

The fifth point was that as the British Expeditionary Force, which had been rescued from Dunkirk, regrouped, re-equipped and came to battle readiness, so it joined the Territorial units already formed into divisions and our defensive strength grew steadily to some thirty or so divisions. The greater our strength, the greater strength was needed by the Germans if they were to have any hope of success, and yet they were simultaneously obliged to cut back on the number and extent of their proposed invasion beaches.

At the same time, the bleeding of coastal vessels and river barges for the invasion was having a terrible effect on the economy not only of Germany but also of the rest of Europe, yet all this time more vessels were being demanded and RAF Bomber Command was constantly niggling away at the assembled shipping, negating every effort to build up a fleet. The result was that there never would be a time when the Germans could assemble enough transport for a sufficiently large force to cross the Channel properly escorted by their navy and supported by the Luftwaffe.

This impasse continued until September 17 when it was at last acknowledged by the Germans that with all their logistic problems, plus the equinoctial gales to be expected in the Channel, Sea Lion was a dead duck. The plan was postponed until the spring of 1941 and, in the interim period, was quietly killed off and buried.

No single factor was responsible for the abandonment of Sea Lion but each individual problem built upon the rest until the weather presented itself as the last straw which broke the Sea Lion's back.

Hitler himself had decreed the final plan and, had the invasion taken place the first wave of troops would have comprised three full infantry divisions, one full mountain division and one parachute division as well the 'leading elements' of four infantry divisions and one mountain division. None of these could hope for reinforcement from the second wave for several days, allowing those thirty British divisions adequate time to move, at the very least, into a holding position while the Royal Navy and Royal Air Force played havoc with the vessels returning to France for refills, thus compounding the shortage of transport vessels. It has since been estimated in both British and German military and naval circles that within one week of the invasion day, supplies and reinforcements would have run out and the last of the invaders would have been obliged to surrender and be rounded up.

Eastbourne would have fallen between the leading elements of 34 Infantry Division landing at Pevensey Bay and the leading elements of 6th Mountain Division landing at Cuckmere Haven, hence the justification for the pounding the town received during the weekend of September 13-15, 1940.

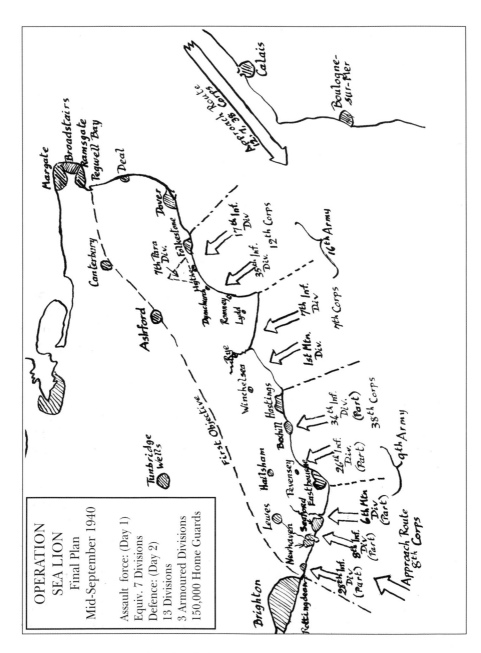

The map contains the following labels:

OPERATION
SEA LION
Final Plan
Mid-September 1940

Assault force: (Day 1)
Equiv. 7 Divisions
Defence: (Day 2)
13 Divisions
3 Armoured Divisions
150,000 Home Guards

Approach Route 32nd Corps
Calais
Boulogne-sur-Mer
Margate
Broadstairs
Ramsgate
Pegwell Bay
Deal
Canterbury
Dover
Folkestone
7th Para Div.
Hythe
Dymchurch
17th Inf. Div.
35th Inf. Div.
12th Corps
16th Army
Romney
Lydd
7th Inf. Div.
7th Corps
1st Mtn. Div.
Ashford
Rye
Winchelsea
Hastings
Bexhill
34th Inf. Div. (Part)
38th Corps
9th Army
Tunbridge Wells
First Objective
Hailsham
Pevensey
26th Inf. Div. (Part)
Eastbourne
6th Mtn Div (Part)
Lewes
Newhaven
Seaford
8th Inf. Div (Part)
Approach Route 8th Corps
Brighton
Rottingdean
28th Inf. Div (Part)

Hitler's final plan for Operation Sea Lion.

CHAPTER ONE
'No Need to Worry'

'I do not think Eastbourne need worry about being bombed in time of war – the attackers, whoever they might be, would not go to the trouble of carrying high explosive bombs for the purpose of bombing Eastbourne.'

Charles Taylor (MP for Eastbourne) speaking to a
meeting of the Junior Primrose League in the spring of 1939.

EASTBOURNE, the 'Empress of Watering Places' as the fashionable publicity blurb would have it, was a completely self-governing county borough before the outbreak of World War II, popular with holiday-makers, still a little Victorian and Edwardian but also alive and forward-looking. A quiet, sedate resort with an air of grandeur and a touch of snobbery.

It seems unbelievable that any enemy would find good reason to bomb such a beautiful place. Indeed, many post-war incomers – notably former Londoners – still believe the town was bombed only by enemy aircraft on the run from London. Had this been so, incidents would have been few, far-between and of little consequence.

To be fair, Charles Taylor was not alone in his beliefs. Just three months previously Eastbourne had been officially designated a 'safety zone' by the Home Office and was warned to expect London evacuees in the event of hostilities breaking out. Fortunately, some people were not prepared to take either Mr Taylor or the Home Office at their word and Air Raid Precautions were advanced apace.

In the early hours of September 1, 1939, the Wehrmacht marched into Poland and Britain was also at war although not yet officially. The blackout became operative and evacuation of London children began on this day.

For three days Eastbourne's railway station saw the arrival of a seemingly unending succession of trains and the well-ordered movement of some 17,000 children and hospital patients to buses, cars and ambulances for transport to billeting centres and on to private homes or hospitals.

At 11am on Sunday, September 3, Prime Minister Neville Chamberlain's infinitely sad voice announced: '. . . therefore a state of war exists between Germany and this country'.

With Eastbourne station still crowded with evacuees, and relays of trains

London evacuee children arrive at Eastbourne station, September 1-3, 1939.

Inspecting a fire crew in 1939 are, centre, from the left, the Mayor of Eastbourne, Arthur Rush, with Charles Taylor MP, Chief Fire Officer SA Phillips and WH Smith, the Chief Constable of Eastbourne.

moving in and out, the air raid sirens were sounded. It was a false alarm sparked off by the movement of an unheralded French aircraft into British airspace. This seemingly unimportant incident had extremely serious repercussions for Eastbourne just over one year later because an edict was made at national level that 'the air raid sirens are not to sound a general alert for the intrusion of single aircraft'. It proved to be a lighted fuse.

Once the evacuees were all in their 'safe havens', billeted and allocated school places, the nation settled comfortably into what one frustrated American journalist dubbed the 'phoney war'. People found the blacked out houses and darkened streets an inconvenience and the whole business of war something of a bore. If any good came of this period it was that people became accustomed to moving around in total blackout and despite what might be considered a perfect environment for burglaries and street robberies, such crime was then as close to non-existent as makes no matter.

March 21, 1940. The town awoke to learn that during the night a merchant ship, the 5,000 ton SS *Barnhill,* had been bombed off Beachy Head sometime between 10.30 and 11pm the previous evening. The *Jane Holland*, Eastbourne's lifeboat (Coxswain Mike Hardy) attended as did a tug from Newhaven.

In the dawn the maimed and drifting vessel made an awesome sight silhouetted against the horizon off the town. Four crewmen died in the explosion and another in hospital. Seven other men were taken to hospital, including the ship's captain, Michael O'Neill. O'Neill might never have been found had not someone reported hearing the ship's bell ringing and called the lifeboat out again. Alec Huggett and Tom Allchorn from the *Jane Holland* took a considerable risk in re-boarding the ship which was blazing so fiercely that its deck plates were red hot, but their efforts were rewarded for they found Captain O'Neill who had suffered a fractured arm, a fractured collarbone and five broken ribs. He had crawled along the hot deck to ring the bell by pulling the rope with his teeth.

Local firemen took trailer pumps aboard the ship and were still fighting

Eastbourne's lifeboat, the Jane Holland, alongside the stricken SS Barnhill.

The SS Barnhill, beached east of Langney Point, after the Eastbourne lifeboat had taken off the crew. Much freight was salvaged by local people.

the fires three days later when, beached just east of Langney Point, the ship broke in two and the firemen were taken off by a fire float.

The fearful sight of that ship ablaze out at sea in the dawn light was unforgettable – but this was merely a beginning.

CHAPTER TWO
The Darkening Picture

'Don't worry, it's one of ours – a Whitley!' A senior cadet
NCO of 54 Squadron, Air Defence Cadet Corps.

O N April 8-9, 1940, the Wehrmacht invaded Denmark and Norway and the phoney war was over. Within a month Germany also attacked Holland, Belgium and Luxembourg. The retreat to Dunkirk and the evacuation of the British Expeditionary Force are a matter of history and legend.

Eastbourne had a hand in these events when the *Jane Holland* and several local fishing and pleasure craft were sent to Dunkirk or St Valery to assist the evacuation. Some were lost, others, like the *Jane Holland* came home with honourable battle scars.

Today the term **South East Region** is taken to mean an area enclosed by two lines running eastward and southward from the vicinity of Oxford. During the war, however, the South East Region was a great deal smaller, conforming to the South Eastern Command which chiefly included Kent, Surrey and Sussex.

With the German army occupying the Channel coast of France and Belgium, the Luftwaffe moving on to airfields in Northern France and the German Navy having access to Dutch, Belgian and French ports the lookout for Britain was bleak but the population remained defiant.

Popular opinion was that the Germans must try an immediate invasion. But, fortunately, their army was overstretched in subduing and occupying France, and had no time for talk of invasion.

However, on May 14, even before the British Expeditionary Force was evacuated from Dunkirk, the new Prime Minister, Winston Churchill, called upon ex-soldiers and others over the age of sixteen to form a new force to be called Local Defence Volunteers to 'observe, report and harass' enemy paratroops should they land and attack. This force, better armed, equipped and trained than the popular image, was later re-named the Home Guard.

Defence works were put in hand and the names of towns and villages were erased from signposts, vehicles and hoardings in the hope of confusing the

Eastbourne's mayor, Councillor Arthur Rush, was at the station in July 1940 to see off the local children who were being evacuated.

enemy. In July the military imposed a seafront curfew on Eastbourne and an edict was made that the town was now part of a defence area and people from outside were prohibited from entering a twenty-mile deep coastal belt. The London evacuees were taken off to other safe havens and 3,000 local school-children followed, to end up in Hertfordshire and Bedfordshire.

July 3, 1940, 16.30 hours. The first bombs to be dropped within the county borough boundary fell near the wreck of the *Barnhill*. They were five or six oil incendiaries and achieved nothing. Indeed, few people recall this as the first incident.

Sunday, July 7, 11.05 hours. There had been no warning sounded when an aircraft flew low over the Upperton district and headed towards the sea. 'Don't worry, it's one of ours – a Whitley!' said a senior cadet NCO of 54 Squadron, Air Defence Cadet Corps. In fact it was a Dornier Do.17 which had been turned away from RAF Wartling radar station and now came for Eastbourne, dropping a stick of bombs down the axis of Whitley Road between the St Philip's Avenue junction and the Avondale Road junction. The first bomb fell at the front of 73 Whitley Road and the last landed in front of

28/30 Whitley Road where it failed to explode. There were ten bombs in all, mostly 50/70kg, but two or three of 250kg were included. (At that time the Do.17 generally lifted about 1,000kg of bombs). Two of the bombs failed to explode.

Robert Woolliams, sixty, was killed outright and William Turner died in hospital three days later. The injured numbered twenty two, nine houses were destroyed and sixty damaged. Two large gas mains in the roadway were fractured and ignited. No warning had been given because of that infamous edict that sirens were not to be sounded for single raiders.

Birchfield's Stores was hit when a Dornier Do17 bombed Whitley Road on July 7, 1940, the town's first taste of war.

This raid was dubbed a 'terror' raid in local newspapers but, in fact, the town had merely been a 'target of opportunity'.

Sunday, July 28, 23.45 hours. A number of bombs were dropped on Long Down. Though London was still not a target for the Luftwaffe, and certainly not by night, enemy aircraft did intrude on pre-invasion reconnaissance operations and, possibly to cover their true task, dropped the bombs almost willy-nilly.

Friday, August 16, 1940, 17.20 hours. A real example of the enemy bombing while 'on the run' took place on this afternoon. A mixed force of German bombers and fighters was driven back from RAF Kenley by defending fighters, and a running fight ensued down to the coast. The Luftwaffe aircraft flew

The wreckage of the Messerschmitt Me110, shot down over Meads on August 16, 1940.

low to put RAF fighters off their 'follow-through' and the bombers jettisoned their bombs to gain speed.

There was a cacophony of aero-engines at full throttle, bombs, cannon and machine guns. Then came a weird, unworldly scream, building up to a fearful crescendo. Suddenly there was comparative silence and the battle swept out over the sea.

The scream was from a Messerschmitt Me110 that had been hit and was breaking up in mid-air. The pilot, Hauptmann Ernst Hollekamp, was killed and thrown out of the plane, his parachute streaming from its pack but failing to deploy. His body struck the roof of Hill Brow School, Meads, and the bulk of the aircraft fell into the grounds of Aldro School. The gunner, who managed to parachute down, was drowned when he fell into the sea.

Some twenty four to twenty six bombs were dropped within the county borough, from just north of Brodrick Road, Hampden Park, to the vicinity of Tutts Barn Lane. In the Hampden Park area no houses were directly hit but there was considerable structural damage.

Three Corporation workmen – Frank Edwards, Harry White and Samuel Henman – who were collecting scrap material for Salvage Week, took cover beneath their lorry as the attack swept over them but a bomb exploded nearby and set the vehicle ablaze. Mr Edwards and Mr White died almost at once and Mr Henman died later in hospital. Remarkably, only two people were injured.

For sticking to their posts throughout the attack and continuing to handle vital calls, two young telephonists at the Hampden Park exchange – Miss ML May, who was nineteen, and Miss MD Sewell, seventeen, were justifiably commended.

As a result of this attack, TR Beckett, proprietor of the *Eastbourne Gazette and Herald* sponsored a Spitfire Fund with the intention of buying a Spitfire to bear the town's name. The (then) princely sum of £5,000 (the value of at least ten good houses) was required to achieve this noble aim and the townspeople responded by giving £6,000 in ten days.

August 17, 1940, 23.30. A wandering Heinkel 111 carrying eight 250kg HE bombs unloaded over France Bottom just east of Beachy Head.

On the nights of August 26, 28, 29 and 30 bombs were again dropped by night wanderers. On the 26th the roof of the Beachy Head Hotel was set alight. On the 28th, nine HE bombs fell at Lower Willingdon but failed to explode. On the 29th, bombs fell between Hampden Park and Friday Street and damage to power cables cut off electricity to surrounding districts, including Newhaven docks. The incident on the 30th succeeded in killing one bullock and wounding another.

> **Blitzkrieg** is a German word meaning lightning war, and it describes fast-moving tank tactics such as were employed in France. The British Press, with its usual skill at mis-using a foreign word, shortened it to **Blitz** and applied it (in particular) to the intensive bombing campaign which was, in fact, a war of attrition – the reverse of lightning war.

Saturday, August 31, 1940, 17.15 hours. An explosion severely damaged 3a Hardwick Mews and injured two women although there had been neither sight nor sound of any aircraft. The intelligence officer of 9th Battalion, Devonshire Regiment examined fragments of the projectile and concluded that they had come from an artillery shell of approximately 4inch calibre.

Mabel Milton, Eastbourne Gazette and Herald's counter clerk,
poses with the collecting boxes for Beckett's Spitfire Fund.

A U-boat was seen to submerge offshore and head westward, pursued by two armed trawlers whose crews confirmed that the submarine had fired its deck gun at the town. (Later, two more shells were fired at Exceat from somewhere off Cuckmere Haven – the proposed landing beach for the German 6th Mountain Division. After the war German photographs and silhouettes of the coastline proved that the shellfire had been a cover for the U-boat's real purpose.)

On Saturday, September 7, 1940, the Luftwaffe finally succeeded in bombing London in daylight and in force and then proceeded to repeat the dose after darkness fell – the London Blitz had begun.

Tuesday, September 10, 1940, saw the issue of a Home Office proclamation inviting all those with no official duties to take advantage of a voluntary evacuation scheme and leave Eastbourne clear for the defenders, should the invasion materialise. During the following few days many took up the offer and

An army intelligence officer of the 9th Battalion Devonshire Regiment
examines a home in Wish Road, damaged after a U-boat shelled
the town on August 31, 1940.

more than a few of them were people already engaged in ARP work - the result of this latter was that a few days later rescue work and reporting of incidents became difficult in the extreme. The stage was now set.

Chapter Three
Friday the Thirteenth

*This was the beginning of the preliminary
bombardment for the expected invasion.*

THE railway station was crowded with people evacuating the town when, without warning, bombs were dropped in two separate areas of the town.

Friday, September 13, 1940, 15.55 hours. A Dornier Do17 carrying one of the two standard loads dropped an oil bomb on Christ Church Junior School, setting the building ablaze and gutting it. A 250kg bomb fell in Seaside near Barden Road, setting fire to a gas main and severely damaging several houses. Another 250kg HE fell in Seaside Recreation Ground blasting a huge crater, and a third HE buried itself in a border at the south west corner of the recreation ground beside the footway along Seaside, where it failed to explode. (This bomb was left undisturbed until 1945 when it was located and detonated).

Over the town centre at least three aircraft were involved. Arlington Road was hit twice as was Old Orchard Road and the Technical Institute and Library (now rebuilt as the Borough Treasurer's offices and Central Library). Hyde Road, Gildredge Road, and West Terrace also suffered. South Street area was also hit half-a-dozen times. The prior evacuation of a number of trained ARP personnel made reporting sketchy and reports by members of the public went a long way to redressing the balance.

Solicitors' offices on the corners of Hyde Road and Gildredge Road were destroyed and many legal papers blown into the air drifted on the wind to fall as far away as Langney and Pevensey Roads.

The total number of bombs on the town centre is variously recorded as eighteen HE and one oil bomb; sixteen HE and one oil; and a second (unexploded) oil bomb is mentioned. The 50kg oil incendiary was pretty unreliable – generally bursting but often failing to ignite.

Four other bombs were dropped in the sea 150 yards from the Cavendish Hotel and this aircraft brings the number of enemy planes employed to at least five.

Casualties were three people killed (including Mary Penfold, sixteen, and Ann Lilian Jones) and thirty injured.

Above: Christ Church Junior School was gutted when a 50kg oil incendiary bomb dropped on it on Friday 13, 1940.

Left: A small bomb tore the front out of this house in Old Orchard Road during the same raid.

This was the beginning of the preliminary bombardment for the expected invasion, and the enemy had only begun to 'get his eye in'.

Saturday, September 14, 1940. During the morning a Dornier Do17 reconnaissance bomber was attacked over the town by two Spitfires and shot down into the sea. This longed-for retaliation lifted the spirits of those left in a town already showing its scars and a thinning population drew breath and waited to see what came next.

At 13.20 hours two Dorniers came in and dropped a total of eight bombs in the Grove Road/College Road/South Street area. An oil bomb in Southfields Road failed to explode and two more bombs in College Road also failed to detonate (one of these may also have been an oil bomb).

Soon afterwards three enemy aircraft came in singly and unloaded sixteen formally recorded bombs in a strip roughly bounded by the seafront and the railway. Four fell short, dropping in the sea off the Burlington Hotel, others struck in front and behind the Burlington Hotel, Elms Avenue, Seaside Road, Susans Road, Pevensey Road, Tideswell Road, South side of All Souls' Church grounds and again near the Church Hall in Longstone Road, Ashford Road and Leaf Road. However, reports made to the police and ARP by the public

This house at the junction of Susans Road and Longstone Road received a direct hit from one of the smaller HE bombs.

record at least six more bombs in this general vicinity.

The timing of the reports gives credence to the familiar recollection that: "They bashed us all afternoon". Again the shortage of ARP personnel (notably Wardens) who had left the town was felt most severely.

The shattered remains of the gardener's cottage in Manor House Grounds, hit on Saturday, September 14, 1940.

Press photographer Harry Deal catches his contemporary, Wilf Bignell (centre) of Eastbourne Gazette and Herald, camera in hand, studying blast damage in Longstone Road on September 14, 1940. War reserve constables gather household belongings.

Two more aircraft dropped a total of eight bombs in the area: The Goffs, High Street, Manor Gardens, Gildredge Park at about 14.30 hours.

At 15.14 hours high flying aircraft dropped thirty HE bombs and twenty four incendiaries. Assuming all the bombs were small, it would require three Dorniers to carry such a number but the likelihood is that there were even more aircraft involved. Recorded bombs fell in Devonshire Park Grounds (five); four in the Firle Road area; seven unexploded bombs in the St Philip's Avenue area, adjacent allotments and Lottbridge Drove. Hundreds of 2kg Thermite incendiaries falling in Meads and in the Archery area were easily dealt with. The bulk of the others were more vaguely located.

The day's activities concluded when three Dorniers attacked the Beachy Head radar station.

Right: The rear wall was torn out at 85 Latimer Road when a bomb exploded in the back garden on Sunday evening, September 15, 1940.

For those involved it was a nightmare of confusions, an afternoon of throbbing aircraft engines, bombs, apprehension, all-pervading dust, debris and the seemingly never-ending attacks. Scratch rescue squads helped out the formal squads (notably that hurriedly formed by Lieutenant Harry White of C Company, Eastbourne Home Guard, who did outstanding work in Firle Road). Generally, there was no panic, no hysteria, just a dour Sussex refusal to be 'druv'. People picked themselves up and got on with the essential work of that grisly afternoon.

Henry Edward Brittain, Wilfrid John Chapman, Miss ID Hipgrave, William H Glen, Eric Channel and Mark Ripley, were killed and Mrs Lottie M Strong died in hospital on October 2 as a result of injuries. Fifty-six people were injured.

Rescuers move out on to the debris after at least one bomb struck the junction of Gildredge Road and Hyde Road on Friday, September 13, 1940.

Undoubtedly the evacuation which so disrupted the ARP effort for a few vital days also served to thin the population to the point that so few people were killed and injured on this unforgettable day.

Air raid warnings were now a weak joke and a new faculty was created – the ability to clearly differentiate between the sounds of enemy and allied aircraft. (A post-war American author declared, categorically, that such a faculty did not exist – fortunately, he was quite wrong). However, the town council put to the government the proposition that if the population were not to be given a General Alert warning of the approach of single aircraft, then at least let them have a local warning. The request was refused as being quite unnecessary.

Anti-aircraft fire was virtually non-existent and the few weapons which existed were mainly 40mm Bofors guns, which had a very limited effective range, and could not hope to hit the Dorniers at the height they were then operating. On this day, too, the Chief Constable, WH Smith, made urgent representations 'to the military' requesting anti-aircraft defences. Alas, they had little or none. The only viable weapons were deployed on London's perimeter.

September 15, 1940. The day now celebrated as Battle of Britain Day – it was 19.05 before three enemy planes returned to the town when some seventeen HE bombs, one oil bomb and a large number of 2Kg Thermite incendiaries were dropped between the Redoubt and Astaire Avenue. No casualties are recorded.

The concensus in the town after this weekend was that we were on our own – and oddly we felt all the stronger for that.

CHAPTER FOUR
Gallantry

*For . . . 36 hours, through daylight and darkness, the rescue
services laboured unstintingly to reach the victims and they did so
in the full knowledge of the UXB lying menacingly so close by.*

UNFORTUNATELY, Hitler and Co failed to inform us that on the morning of September 17 the threatened invasion had been postponed until the spring of 1941 but the postponement was soon obvious when, following the blows of the weekend of 13-15, we were not greatly troubled for a further week. Before the lull, on **September 16,** and for the first time, an enemy aircraft running for home after an abortive approach to London dropped a number of HE and incendiaries on the Crumbles at about 04.40 hours.

Bomb damage at Queen's Crescent.

Sunday, September 22, 1940, 17.15 hours. Our private squabble with the Luftwaffe again came to life with a long series of air raids having no connection with the defunct invasion and serving no observable military purpose. Four HE bombs fell in the Queen's Crescent area, one outside 64 Queen's Crescent, one at rear of Queen's Road, one in disused ground between the rear of Queen's Road and the Queen Alexandra Cottage Homes and one, which failed to explode, in allotments fronting Seaside opposite the homes – this latter remained in situ until inadvertently turned up by an excavator many years later. Another salvo of bombs landed near Whitley Road bridge and again one failed to explode. The absence of an oil incendiary in these two loads suggests that two Junkers Ju88s were employed. In all, four people were injured, three houses were destroyed and 20 badly damaged.

Monday, September 23, 1940, 11.50 hours. A total of twenty eight bombs were dropped by a number of aircraft approaching singly. Two Ju88s dropped eight HE bombs in the area Cavendish Bridge, the railway station and The Avenue and two Dornier Do17s dropped ten each between Langney Road/Bourne Street and Avondale Road/Nevill Road. At 16.35 hours a further eight bombs were dropped in the general area, damaging the railway and closing the station – accurate locations for these bombs are difficult to come by since the ARP file has gone astray, however, at least one bomb fell as far afield as the grounds of Compton Place. Twenty three people were injured in the day's attacks. The amount of property destroyed and damaged was considerable, and the Bourne Street/Langney Road junction soon earned the title 'Hell Fire Corner'.

Tuesday, September 24, 1940, 02.20 hours. Another bomber in retreat from London jettisoned two oil bombs and three HE in the Gildredge Road, Grove Road, Saffrons Road, Meads Road area. One HE exploded on the cricket table on the Saffrons, a UXB fell in Compton Place Road, another in Saffrons Road outside Caffyns Garage, an oil bomb in Gildredge Road burst but failed to ignite and another landed in a Grove Road cellar where it failed to burst. At 07.00 hours the bomb in Saffrons Road exploded, damaging both the garage and the west wing of the Town Hall opposite. No one was hurt.

Thursday, September 26, 1940, 16.17 hours. The daylight attackers returned

The bomb that fell in Old Orchard Road on September 26 1940 blew this crater in the road and fractured a water main. Damage to homes was light.

Junction of Cavendish Place and Tideswell Road, September 28 1940. An emergency amputation was performed to free Peggy Harland .

and two aircraft dropped seven HE and one oil bomb. One HE struck platforms 3 and 4 of the railway station and another hit the tracks near Cavendish Bridge, a UXB landed at the rear of St Leonards Road and the oil bomb set fire to a car in Commercial Road. An HE exploded in Old Orchard Road, another in Arlington Road where two UXBs were also located. One of the UXBs in Arlington Road exploded at 20.46 hours. At about the same time as this raid, some 20 bombs were dropped on the Downs but failed to explode.

Two people were killed and two injured.

Friday, September 27, 1940, 05.47 hours. 'Night owls' abandoning a London raid jettisoned 12 HE between Hampden Park and Friday Street – one was a UXB. Total casualties were two bullocks dead and two more injured!

Saturday, September 28, 1940. The start of a weekend of sheer gallantry and courage . . . at 17.48 and again at 18.06 attacks were made by single aircraft, each dropping four bombs. Four HE (2 UXBs) were dropped from Ashford Square, beside Cavendish Bridge and into Upper Avenue. The other four bombs, however, instigated the most famous rescue of the war in Eastbourne. One oil bomb at rear of 87 Tideswell Road; one HE demolished 69/71 Cavendish Place and 127 Tideswell Road; a UXB fell at the rear of Mansfield's Garage close behind the last damage; one HE demolished 40, 42, 44 Bourne Street.

As a result of the bomb in Cavendish Place, several people were trapped in cellars beneath masses of debris from shattered shops and flats above, their ordeal terrible as they waited for the rescuers to reach them.

For the next 36 hours, through daylight and darkness, the rescue services laboured unstintingly to reach the victims and they did so in the full knowledge of the UXB lying menacingly so close by. The rescue squads had to tunnel into the treacherous debris and then hack their way through obstructing concrete, their work being hampered by a burst water main which could only be kept in check by continuous pumping by the fire brigade. Some men, exhausted by their efforts, were removed, taken to hospital, recovered and returned to the task. None had a single thought for himself.

Among those trapped was a seventeen-year-old Hankham girl, Peggy Harland, who was pinned down by her ankles. In great pain and unable to move, Peggy nevertheless remained cheerful and even managed to keep up the spirits of her rescuers as they toiled desperately to reach her and her companions. Alas, when it was possible to examine her closely, it was realised it would be impossible to free her by conventional means and doctors decided to amputate Peggy's legs there and then.

In the most dreadful conditions of lack of space, debris and dust, amid anaesthetic fumes and the ever-present threat of the unexploded bomb, the operation was performed and it was at last possible to bring Peggy out into the air where she was removed to hospital. Two days later Peggy Harland died. For her gallantry, Peggy – a Girl Guide with the 1st Stone Cross Company – was posthumously awarded the Girl Guides' Gilt Cross (known as the Guides' VC) as a tribute to the magnificent courage and cheerfulness she displayed.

Those who died in this attack were: Stanley Giles, Peggy Harland, Olive Giles and Myrtle Wilkinson. Fourteen other people were injured.

Wednesday, October 2, 1940, 06.45 hours. An early bird Dornier Do17 called and dropped an oil bomb on 16 Upperton Gardens, which was gutted; one HE fell in gardens opposite 11-17 Upperton Gardens; a second behind 9 Upperton Gardens and another on Hadley House on the corner of Upperton Road and The Avenue. There were no deaths but twelve people were injured.

At 16.58 hours that same day, fifteen bombs were dropped in the area of Silverdale Road, South Street, Carlisle Road, Blackwater Road, Grange Road and College Road (this neighbourhood was then known as the College Area not Lower Meads, as latter-day estate agents imply). The number of bombs is unusual and difficult to account for. Officially only 'a high-flying aircraft' is recorded when two, or even three would have

Gallantry rewarded

So impressive was the September 28 rescue operation, and the gallantry shown all round, that fourteen awards were made.

Chief Officer SA Phillips of the Fire Brigade was awarded an MBE. AE Blackmer, EH May, EF Stevens, EL Turney (all from rescue squads) were each awarded the George Medal. Commendations went to Dr J Fenton (Medical Officer of Health), Dr RM Barron, Dr AH Snowball, RV Harvey (rescue), Sub-Officer SN Waymark (fire brigade), EA Homewood (fire brigade) Police Constable RT Jeffrey, HM Barnes (senior Air Raid Warden) and AJ Barkham (Air Raid Warden).

It is a matter for profound regret that Eastbourne Council has not yet seen fit to place so much as a plaque in the Town Hall recording for posterity the names of these heroes and heroine.

been needed to carry such a load.

Thomas H Gurr was killed in the grounds of the Convent of the Nativity and Harry Shadbolt in South Street. Two people were injured.

Again, at 20.10 hours, a Dornier Do17, its crew not fancying the trip to London, unloaded in the St Anthony's area. Two HE exploded, there was one UXB and one oil bomb. No casualties. Slight damage to houses.

Damaged homes in Northbourne Road.

Sunday, October 6, 1940, 10.30 hours. A lone Dornier Do17 crossed the coast near Beach Road, released its bombs but did not turn away immediately.

A 250kg bomb took the front out of the Berkeley Club in Trinity Place.

Three HE fell on or near 134 and 152 Northbourne Road and an oil bomb struck the pavement outside number 112. Only one person was injured.

Monday, October 7, 1940, 10.40 hours. Another Do17 flying at about 1,500 feet, dropped one HE at the rear of 6 Bedford Grove, another hit 81/83 Enys Road, a third failed to explode in a passage between Enys and Arundel Roads and an oil bomb hit 18 Carew Road. Five people were injured.

Bobbys, now Debenhams, suffered a near miss at its Lismore Road frontage.

Tuesday, October 8, 1940. Two raids came later in the day. At 16.15 hours an HE fell in Lismore Road next to Bobby's (Debenhams) frontage, one oil bomb beside 5 Lismore Road did little damage but another oil bomb on the Oak Cabin Restaurant (19 Terminus Road before re-numbering), caused a large fire. A second HE fell in the back garden of a house in North Street but failed to explode – it was later dug out by a Bomb Disposal Squad.

Carol W Lawry was injured and died in hospital next day. Three people were injured.

The second raid also included two oil bombs one of which struck Grand Parade between the Carpet Gardens and the western end of the Burlington Hotel – it burst but failed to ignite; the other fell behind 10 Cavendish Place but its effect is not recorded. One 'large' HE fell on the roadway and wall at Findon House, Hartington Place, and the other on the lawns of the Berkeley Club, Trinity Place. Rumour had it that this raider was shot down into the sea.

The last of the day's raids was made by two Junkers Ju88s when official records report a single raider dropped: one HE bomb on Cavendish Bridge; another on sidings next to Pickford's warehouse; one on the main line and one on the coal wharf plus four HE on railway line. Experienced eye-witnesses, however, reported two Junkers Ju88s making 'shallow dive' attacks and this suggests four more bombs whose records are lost.

CHAPTER FIVE
Spreading the Gospel

*As the bombs fell, the faraway Regional Controller
had the general All Clear sounded!*

H ITLER had, by now, ditched Operation Sea Lion – yet still the battering of the south coast continued and there was little respite for the people of Eastbourne.

October 10, 1940, 15.30 hours. A high-flying Junkers Ju88, travelling west to east, dropped a widely-spaced stick of four HE bombs. One, which failed to explode, fell in the garden of 23 Park Avenue; one was a direct hit on Mayfair, Kings Drive; the third fell on a playing field near the west entrance to Hampden Park and the fourth was a direct hit on St Mary's Church, Decoy Drive. This bomb went through the roof and demolished the building, leaving only the east wall with its attached bell still standing. The church hall which, only a short time earlier, had been filled with diners as a communal feeding centre, was severely damaged. Parts of hymn and prayer books from the church were

All that remains of St Mary's Church, Hampden Park after a direct hit by a 250kg bomb.

blown into the westerly breeze and scattered over a wide area – even east of the railway line. In all this, only one person was injured.

Friday, October 11, 1940, 12.00 hours. Two very high-flying Junkers Ju88s each dropped two sticks of four HE. One, a UXB, fell in a brickyard near Hampden Park; one fell on marshland east of the railway and 'three' fell between the railway and Rodmill (three is probably a miscount because of many earlier craters). The second bomber dropped a UXB at the rear of 15 Firle Road; one HE on rear of 94/96/98 Sydney Road; one HE in the road near the junction of Hartfield Road and Upperton Gardens; one HE on Saffrons Cricket Ground.

Several men removing furniture from one of the three houses in Sydney Road were trapped beneath debris but John Hollands and John Appleby were quickly on the scene and despite danger to themselves from falling debris, went in and extricated the trapped men. During this work, Mr Hollands was injured.

Sidney Alfred Hutchinson was dead when taken from the wreckage; Frank Hurd and Charles Langford died later in hospital. Two others were injured, one seriously.

Total casualties were three dead, five injured. Mr Hollands was later awarded the Order of the British Empire and Mr Appleby was commended.

Sunday, October 13, 1940, 09.35 hours. Reports claim eleven bombs were dropped in the Brodrick Road area. One HE in Brodrick Lane (now part of Brodrick Road); one HE in new Hampden Park School grounds; five HE (two UXBs) on land east of Brodrick Lane; four HE (one UXB) on land west of school. The total of eleven bombs is probably the result of a miscount due to several older craters in the area. There were no casualties.

Monday, October 14, 1940, 22.03 hours. A night wanderer jettisoned a load of 2Kg incendiaries and two oil bombs near Belle Tout.

Wednesday, October 16, 1940, 02.05 hours. Another aircraft jettisoned two HE between Kings Drive and the railway.

Thursday, October 17, 1940, 19.15 hours. This attack has proved very difficult to rationalise since the number of bombs dropped coincides with the loads of none of the usual crop of aircraft. An HE bomb near the Archery failed to detonate; there were two HE near Rodmill; a possible UXB was reported to have fallen somewhere between St Anthony's and The Hydneye; one HE fell near the junction of Kings Drive and Decoy Drive; and another HE (UXB) fell in the garden at rear of 34 Brampton Road. The latter bomb reportedly buried itself 20ft into the ground and took three months to dig out. It was said to be the largest dropped in the borough up to that time and is estimated to have been of 1,000kg calibre (2,200lb approx). At that time the Heinkel 111, which was designed to carry eight 250kg bombs in internal racks, was modified to carry the larger bomb on an external rack and, if such an aircraft had carried that bomb it was, in theory, capable of also carrying four 250kg bombs. The Dornier Do217 was also capable of carrying these bombs. The records show a total of six bombs.

Neither casualties nor damage are recorded.

October 19, 1940, 23.45 hours. An unidentified enemy aircraft made four machine-gun attacks on the Gas Works and, on the third run, punctured Number Three gasholder and ignited the gas. The fire brigade attended and Eastbourne Gas Company workmen carried out emergency repairs while enemy aircraft were still in the vicinity. No one was hurt. One interesting feature of this incident was that it gave the lie to all those 'dismal Jimmies' who had predicted that if ever a gasholder was hit it would explode with dire consequences over a very wide area.

Tuesday, October 22, 1940, 10.20 hours. An aircraft reported as 'a Dornier' approached at about 1,500ft and dropped eleven bombs – mixed HE and anti-personnel (not all were fully recorded). Eleven 'mixed bag' bombs is one more than one of the two standard loads

Langney Road on October 22, 1940, when an unusual number of bombs were dropped.

for a Dornier Do 17 and is one short of the other standard load of three Do17s. One HE scored a direct hit on 107 Langney Road; one HE (some claim two) demolished 111 and 113 Langney Road; another fell in the centre of Langney Road just west of Bourne Street junction and fractured a gas main. Two people were trapped by an HE that fell at the rear of 99 Langney Road, and one died before rescue squads could reach the couple. There was also a direct hit on 34 Bourne Street, and a UXB was suspected in 110 Langney Road.

It is most likely that the unrecorded anti-personnel bombs were the smaller type of HE fused to detonate on or just before impact, scattering splinters wide and at a low level. These bombs inherited the title of 'daisy-cutters' from certain types of shells of the Great War. Photographs taken at the time by Wilf Bignell show bomb splinter holes very low down on house walls in Bourne Street.

The broken gas main in Langney Road cut off the supply of gas to Beckett's premises where the next day's *Eastbourne Gazette* was being typeset. Despite this being a press day, the potential disaster of having no gas for heating the printing metal was circumvented and the paper came out on time.

Three people were killed in this attack: F Baker, Hans Jensen, and John Harrison Bontoft, a well-known local entertainer, who died in hospital.

Fifteen were injured, including a man repairing a Langney Road house roof damaged in an earlier raid. Mr Parsons, a first aid worker, climbed onto the roof via a window of the house to attend to the casualty until the fire brigade could bring him down.

Friday, October 25, 1940, 16.15 hours. A formation of enemy aircraft crossing the town at a great height was intercepted by RAF fighters and some of the bombers jettisoned their bombs. One HE fell on 4-6 The Goffs; another in the garden between 4 and 6 Lewes Road; a third on Scott's Nurseries, Gorringe Road and a fourth on allotments behind 111 Ringwood Road. There was a direct hit on Mark Martin's premises behind 75 Ashford Road; and three HE fell on grassland at Rodmill Farm, straddling Kings Drive. Six people were injured in this attack.

As the bombs fell, the faraway Regional Controller had the general All Clear sounded!

Whenever animals were trapped by debris, RSPCA Inspector E (Teddy) Winn was on the scene, frequently placing his own life at risk in his efforts to save the animals. He is seen here rescuing a dog from the wreckage of a house in The Goffs. After the rescue he visited the owner in hospital to cheer her with the news of her dog's return to safety.

A love of animals and tremendous bravery were not Teddy's only assets. He also had a flair for amusing the human residents whenever there was a concert or party requiring entertainers.

His mimes in particular are still fondly remembered by those who knew him.

Another brave man.

CHAPTER SIX
The Pub Crawl

He got to his feet and headed for the Cavendish Hotel saloon
bar for a much-needed drink . . . an unexploded bomb, however,
had beaten him to the door – but not yet ordered!

T HE last raid of any consequence in 1940 remains a talking point to this
day among those who were there, and who remember the strange
sequence of events. But first, more death and devastation was to come.

Saturday, October 26, 1940, 08.50 hours. A Dornier Do17 dropped four
bombs: one, an oil bomb, struck the roof of a train in the station but failed to
ignite; an HE lodged under another carriage of the train failed to explode;
and two more which fell in Kilburn Terrace were also UXBs. Unfortunately,
only one of the two in Kilburn Terrace was located at the time.

**Sergeant Hoare of the bomb disposal squad had defused the bomb which
was found in one house only for the unknown bomb to explode and kill both
him and Police Sergeant Owens, who was the town's Bomb Reconnaisance
Officer.**

During rescue efforts, the defused bomb was found and a Royal Engineers
corporal decided to tow it out with the aid of a corporation lorry. When work
resumed, the bodies of the two sergeants were recovered. In all, four people
died on this day.

Six more attacks of little consequence occurred on **October 29**, **November
5, 6, 7, 8** and at 04.45 hours on the **10th.**

Sunday, November 10, 1940 10.10 hours. A number of Dornier Do17s, operating singly, came in off the sea just east of the pier, one dropping at least ten
bombs from the Albion Hotel (now The Carlton Hotel) to Langney Road. The
Lion Inn was destroyed, the licensee killed and his wife injured. Among other
structural damage, gas mains and sewers at the Ceylon Place/Bourne Street
junction; near 41 Ceylon Place; and 79 Pevensey Road were fractured. A second raider dropped another stick of ten bombs from Langney Road to
Dennis Road (now Dursley Road), ripping the heart out of the little streets of
houses just behind the Rose and Crown public house. Eight more bombs were

Charles Rich, landlord of the Lion Inn, was killed, and his wife was injured when a bomb destroyed the pub on Sunday morning, November 10, 1940.

dropped on marshland behind Astaire Avenue and at least four more in the sea just 200yd offshore.

Despite all these bombs, only two people – Charles Rich and Mrs Laura Hudson – were killed, and five people injured.

Monday, November 11, 1940, 02.05 hours. A 'night wanderer seeking amusement' flew low and machine-gunned the railway engine sheds before heading home.

Some of the early damage to battered Bourne Street.

Tuesday, November 12, 1940, 14.20 hours. A low-flying aircraft (recorded as a Dornier Do17 but actually a Junkers Ju88) machine-gunned the streets as it headed east before turning and heading out to sea. **19.30 hours.** An enemy aircraft – probably another Do17 – dropped a long stick of bombs from the northern end of Victoria Drive, across the Old Town council housing estate to Victoria Gardens. Most of the bombs – which all failed to explode – fell in gardens, but one struck the roof of 16 Central Avenue and passed right through the house to bury itself in the scullery floor. As a precaution, 400 people were evacuated from their homes while the bombs were examined and declared safe. A rumour ran rife that these bombs had been made in Czechoslovakia and deliberately sabotaged. Alas, the likelihood is that the bomb aimer simply forgot to select 'live' before releasing them.

Friday, November 15, 1940, 19.10 hours. Ten bombs were recorded as falling in a stick in the Ratton, Babylon Plantation, Willingdon Road, Kings Drive area. Casualties were few and light largely because, then, much of the area was uninhabited grassland.

November 22, 1940, 14.10 hours. This, the last raid of consequence in 1940, remains to this day a talking point with surviving residents. Officially, a single enemy aircraft emerged from low cloud over Upperton and dropped a stick of bombs from the railway station to the Cavendish Hotel. This raid became known as The Pub Crawl because the first clearly visible bomb damage was to the Gildredge Hotel in Terminus Road and, at the other end of the stick, an unexploded 50kg bomb was found lodged through a door panel of the saloon bar of the Cavendish Hotel (the bar entrance was then in Devonshire Place and opposite the Duke of Devonshire's statue).

In fact, it is pretty certain three separate aircraft were involved, the first dropping a salvo of four bombs: one HE on Platform One and the railway track at the station; one HE on the rear wing of the Gildredge Hotel; one directly on 135 Terminus Road (now 41/43) and one HE in the roadway outside Plummer Roddis, Terminus Road (now C & H Fabrics).

Another aircraft dropped a four-bomb salvo – one HE on the east side of Hyde Gardens near Cornfield Road; one in Cornfield Road opposite the west side of Hyde Gardens; two behind the east side of Cornfield Road.

The third bomber carried the ten assorted bomb load of the Dornier Do17. One HE fell behind the east side of Cornfield Road; one in the garden at the rear of 1 Seaside Road (now Trinity Trees); one at the front of 2 Seaside Road; one at the rear of Hanburies Hotel, 2 Devonshire Place; one at the front of 6 Devonshire Place; one at the rear of 6 Devonshire Place; one at the junction of Devonshire Place and Compton Street; one (UXB) in the Devonshire Place

Above, Platform One at the railway station after the bomb fell.
Left, the end of the Pub Crawl – an unexploded bomb in the door of the Cavendish Hotel.

doorway of the saloon bar of the Cavendish Hotel; one on the beach near the bandstand. Finally, there was much talk of a bomb in the sea and this would complete a full load.

One man caught in the open in Devonshire Place when the bombs fell, dived for cover in the gutter and then, as the dust and debris settled, he got to his feet and realised the Cavendish saloon bar should still be open and there was just time for a much-needed stiff drink. He reached the head of the steps leading down to the saloon bar door, turned and – there was the unexploded bomb which had beaten him to the bar door but had not yet ordered!

Mrs MA Graham was killed and ten people were injured – another minor miracle.

November 23, December 9 and December 13. Bombers abandoning sorties on London, jettisoned bombs within the borough boundaries with negligible effect. Then, three months to the day since the town's ordeal began, there came a respite which was to last almost three months more.

March 11, 1941, 22.06 hours. Battle resumed when enemy aircraft aborted a raid on London and dropped four HE bombs on Green Street smallholdings and four HE at Hodcombe Farm. No damage or casualties were reported.

March 12, 1941, 20.03 hours. Another wanderer jettisoned five bombs between Bullock Down and Warren Hill and neither casualties nor damage are recorded.

March 12, 1941, 21.25 hours. An aircraft (probably a Heinkel 111) made a low-level run across the town and dropped eight bombs. They fell in the roadway outside 124/126 Northbourne Road, fracturing mains; on waste ground (now council housing) at the junction of Churchdale and Southbourne Roads; on the workshops of the Corporation Bus Depot, Churchdale Road; at the junction of Rylstone and Halton Roads and on the foreshore opposite the Angles Hotel (now the Majestic).

One bomb passed through the eight inch concrete of Ecmod Road and exploded with a muffled bang. A resident, concerned for a neighbour, left his house in the blackout to cross the road, only to find himself walking 'up hill'. He had found where the bomb had lifted the concrete *en masse*. No casualties were sustained.

March 13, 1941, 20.53 hours. An incoming bomber, attacked by night fighters, jettisoned its bombs which included 'Molotov Breadbaskets' (HE bombs with 2kg incendiaries mounted in a tandem container over the tail). An estimated 200-300 2kg incendiaries fell on the rear of the gas works and fields beyond. Four bombs that failed to explode fell in the fields towards Hampden Park. Incendiaries that fell on gas works buildings were extinguished by the gas works platoon attached to C Company, 21st (Eastbourne) Battalion, Sussex Home Guard. A nearby piggery was also damaged by fire. A UXB near Brampton Road was exploded at 2pm on April 13, 1941 but there is no record of the others being dealt with. Nor is there any record of casualties or other damage.

March 28, 1941, 09.39 hours. A Ju88 crossed the town at about 500ft and dropped four bombs in the Archery area, only to return a few minutes later in a machine-gun attack. There was a direct hit by an HE bomb on 17, 19, 21 Churchdale Road; one HE in the rear gardens of the same houses; one HE direct hit on 23 and 25 Willoughby Crescent; and one HE in the Archery Recreation Ground near the junction of Southbourne Road and Seaside. This latter bomb had bounced from the roadway in Churchdale Road, a distance of some 300 yards, an occurrence that was not uncommon. Both British and Germans bombs used delay fuses of about ten seconds or so when bombs were to be dropped from low altitude. This gave the aircraft time to get clear of the blast so, when such a bomb – still virtually horizontal – struck a hard flat surface it could bounce surprisingly long distances before exploding.

Three large bombs cut a swathe through houses in Churchdale Road
and Willoughby Crescent and a fourth bounced to within 100yd
of St Andrew's Church before exploding.

Mrs A Guy, Mrs AM Cooper and Brian Fly, aged six, were killed. Twenty five people were injured.

During this raid six houses were completely demolished and others were severely damaged.

April 3, 9, 11, 19, May 9 and 11. Abandoned sorties against London accounted for attacks by single aircraft which caused little or no significant damage and inflicted no casualties.

Sunday, May 11, 05.19 hours. A Heinkel 111 dropped eight bombs that fell in a stick from the house called Aubrey in Kings Drive to the approximate location of the present hospital roundabout. Aubrey was hit directly as was Hereward, also in Kings Drive. A gas main was fractured and ignited in Park Avenue but otherwise there was some damage but no casualties.

May 24, 1941, 18.30 hours. A Ju88 flew low across the Archery area and dropped four HE bombs: One in gardens at rear of 18/20 Churchdale Road; one on the rear of 11 Channel View Road; one in the garden at the rear of St Elmo, 27 Channel View Road; and one on the beach roughly opposite Princes Park bowling greens. One of the bombs which landed in Channel View Road had first struck the road beside the well-known Archery Tavern (now under its third change of name – The Castle) and bounced over the sewage pumping station opposite. Fifteen people were injured in this attack.

June 7, 1941, 03.30 hours. A single raider approached the town from the north, came in low with his engines throttled back and dropped four bombs before revving-up and climbing away hard. One was a direct hit on 21 The Avenue; one fell in the back gardens of 22 and 23 The Avenue; one landed in the back garden of 19 St Leonards Road; and one was a direct hit on 21 St Leonards Road. No one was killed but twelve people were injured. This site was cleared right through from The Avenue to St Leonards Road and has since been redeveloped with flats.

There then followed a much-needed holiday from the attentions of the Luftwaffe and, for almost eleven months, we lived in relative peace but with eyes and ears forever cocked for the sound of enemy aircraft. Nor were we the only ones to be misled – people who had evacuated the town in 1940 now began to trickle back bringing stories of the hardships they had endured in

The scene of devastation in Channel View Road.

their retreats. Alas the Luftwaffe was re-thinking its policy and tactics and the price for Eastbourne and Eastbournians was to be high.

BUGBEAR

T HE night was moonless, overcast and pitch black. Two French Canadian sentries of Le Régiment de Maisonneuve were patrolling along the cat-walk behind the beach near Pevensey Bay village when one of them caught the unmistakable sound of movement on the shingle. Alert now, they searched the blackness for some further clues and saw shadowy figures slipping quickly down the beach towards the sea. They opened fire on the figures and what they took to be a rubber dinghy. The muzzle flash of their rifles effectively night-blinded them and they could see no more detail of the beach scene. Suddenly, a light winked well out to sea, off the bay.

The sentries reported the incident and turned out their full patrol, the commander of which notified battalion headquarters. It was 19.55 hours on February 4, 1942.

The battalion notified the headquarters of Canadian 5th Infantry Brigade and also the Black Watch, the Royal Highlanders of Canada, at Eastbourne. The code word AFLOAT was issued, with PEVENSEY to locate the incident. The 5th Brigade stood-to the whole brigade and three adjacent Home Guard battalions in case the incursion proved to be at some strength. In Eastbourne, the Black Watch had also reported seeing the lights off Pevensey Bay, confirming the report of the French Canadians.

Two hours passed during which some 6,000 men – Canadians and Home Guards – waited to see just what the enemy had in mind, but as he made no other landing attempt everyone was stood down, leaving an unanswered question: What was the reconnaissance party hoping to achieve?

The answer came at Easter – April 5 and 6. An entry in the war diary of the Canadian 5th Infantry Brigade for April 2, 1942, mentions that information was received from 2nd Division that there were concentrations of enemy paratroops and flame-thrower units on the French coast. As a result, all units in the coastal area were put on stand-to and all patrols and guards doubled. Anti-raid precautions were checked and all vital points patrolled.

The entry for April 3, states that two senior RAF officers visited the Brigade headquarters to discuss the defences of the RAF-AMC (Radar) Stations at Pevensey and Wartling. That afternoon, the Brigadier and his Intelligence Officer made an inspection of existing defences and arranged for further barbed-wiring and siting of gun pits.

In the April 3 entry of the war diary of the Black Watch at Eastbourne, reference is made to a telephone call received at 20.00 hours the previous evening from the Brigade Major who said a raid by seaborne and/or airborne troops was expected on the RAF Station at PEVENSEY. (Such an assault would require the attackers to be withdrawn by sea, hence the February reconnaissance(s) at Pevensey Bay.) The carrier platoon (tracked Bren gun carriers) and duty company stood-to. Stand-down was at 07.26 hours.

The diary entry for April 4 states that the acting GOC 2nd Canadian Division had announced that a raid was expected on April 5 or 6 (Easter weekend) and that all precautions must be rehearsed. He also said the announcement originated from the RAF and that a German parachute battalion was ready in France. On April 5 the anti-raid position was given for OPERATION BUGBEAR PEVENSEY.

Unfortunately, many Londoners, seemingly believing the war was virtually 'over', and as the weather was so good, decided to spend Easter at the seaside – also in the belief that as a seaside resort, Eastbourne would open its arms to them. In coming down they also breached the twenty mile exclusion zone for visitors.

There was no extra food for these people, very little accommodation available, they could not go on to the beach and, all in all, had made a terrible error.

The Canadian general, fortunately, kept his news very much to his own troops and 'demonstrated' his force in the vicinity of RAF Wartling with the result that the enemy, with barely a tenth of his strength, decided not to come after all and the Londoners were spared much anguish as a result.

A Focke-Wulf FW190 in a ditch in Lottbridge Drove, shot down by a Canadian Bren-gunner on August 26, 1942.

Photographer Harry Deal pictured by Wilf Bignell with the remains of the twin engined Messerschmitt ME110 fighter that fell into the grounds of Aldro School after being shot down on August 16, 1940, over Meads. The pilot's body fell on to the roof of nearby Hill Brow School while the gunner parachuted into the sea and drowned.

This 500kg bomb dropped on Friday, June 4, 1943, passed through St Saviour's Vicarage and into the church without exploding. It was later defused.

St. John's Church

CHAPTER SEVEN
The Fighter Bombers

'Though it is established fact that Allied aircraft machine-gunned civilian targets in Germany, there is no true record of German aircraft ever machine-gunning civilian targets.' American author of a book on the Allied bombing offensive.

ALMOST eleven months passed, during which the Luftwaffe left Eastbourne alone; then a new threat erupted.

MAY 4, 1942, 13.55 hours. Nine Messerschmitt Me109 fighter-bombers, each carrying a 250kg high explosive bomb, found their way across the Channel, lifted up over Beachy Head and, turning, swept down across the town with cannon and machine guns blazing.

One scored a direct hit on St John's Church, Meads, and the ensuing fire completely gutted the building and finished the work of the blast. A second bomb was a direct hit on 15, 17 and 19 Willingdon Road; a third struck the railway station platforms; a fourth hit 1 and 2 Commercial Road; one HE on the railway near Cavendish Bridge and a fifth fell on coal wharf sidings at the rear of Winter Road (now Winchcombe Road). Other bombs struck the east wing of the Cavendish Hotel, trapping a number of RAF personnel billeted there, the locomotive sheds and a gasholder.

Mrs Henrietta Wise, Mrs Winifred Matthews, Mrs Mary Richardson, Claude Benjamin and one other were killed. Thirty-six people were injured.

Two UXBs were also suspected but were swiftly discounted.

Alec Huggett, a local fisherman, and Micky Andrews, a local fishmonger assisting as crew, were fishing offshore in a simple wooden fishing smack when this raid occurred and as the enemy planes turned for

The shattered east wing of the Cavendish Hotel.

'During a bombing attack on Eastbourne today, Luftwaffe fighter-bombers also shot up an armed trawler offshore.' William Joyce (Lord Haw-Haw), presenting the news in English from Germany soon after 9 pm on May 4, 1942. After the war Joyce was hanged for treason, but had Eastbournians been able to lay hands on him that day he would have been decorating a lamp-standard long before the war ended.

the run home, one or more of them fired on the vessel. Micky Andrews lost a leg and was badly wounded in the stomach, and Alec Huggett received head wounds, but both men survived.

A notable feature of this raid (apart from it being the first of the fighter-bomber raids) was that almost every bomb did serious damage. Militarily the railway was a legitimate target and was heavily hit. The gas holder was also a fair target. The Cavendish Hotel, at that time, housed RAF personnel (trainee navigators) and was also a legitimate target (assuming the enemy was aware of its significance). In general, too, the fighter pilots with their medium capacity delayed-action bombs seemed to have a better aim than the bomb-aimers in the standard medium bombers.

This raid caused a rapid re-think among those imprudent evacuees who, lulled into a false sense of security, had returned prematurely.

May 7, 1942, 15.11 hours. Four Messerschmitt Me109s, each carrying one 250kg bomb, attacked with cannon and machine guns firing. One bomb scored direct hit on 7, 9, 11 Victoria Place and others hit the railway goods yard, coal wharf sidings and the sea wall. The attackers swung back over Beachy Head, firing on the way at the Royal Naval Shore Signal Station and the Royal Observer Corps post. A War Department launch was also fired upon and disabled, two of the crew being wounded.

In the town, Mr J Payne was killed and thirty one people were injured.

Bomb damage at Victoria Place – now the sea-ward end of Terminus Road. The site was the last in the town to be fully redeveloped after the war.

The Cuckoo at last!

On June 6, 1942, the long-running battle with the Home Office to secure a local warning system was at last resolved when air raid sirens were modified so that for a purely local alert the two notes which made up the familiar howling could be separated to create a cuckoo-like sound – hence the local term 'a cuckoo warning'.

There is a story, possibly apocryphal, of a Home Office representative addressing a meeting at Eastbourne Town Hall to explain why a local warning system was quite unnecessary when the Luftwaffe paid one of its unheralded visits at low altitude. Eastbourne got its local warning!

August 11, 1942, 23.00 hours. Besides being Eastbourne's most severe night raid, this attack later prompted many questions and recriminations about the ill-fated Dieppe Raid eight days later.

At about 11pm the sound of approaching enemy bombers provoked no undue alarm – night raiders generally were on their way elsewhere and only jettisoned bombs found their way into the borough boundary during the hours of darkness. Then flares illuminated the town and locals realised this was to be no ordinary night.

An uncertain number of medium bombers attacked the Upperton, Grove Road and the Eastbourne College area (the latter area now erroneously dubbed Lower Meads by estate agents). Some fifty seven high explosive bombs and 2,000+ 2kg Thermite incendiary bombs were dropped, the incendiaries being fitted with burster charges to scatter flaming fragments and deter fire-fighters, amateur and professional.

High explosive bombs made direct hits on: an air raid shelter at Roborough, The Avenue (then used as an annexe to the Princess Alice Hospital), killing eight Canadian RAMC men and injuring three; on Roborough playing field; in the front garden of 13 Upper Avenue; on the drive of 13 Upper Avenue; opposite 7 Lewes Road; at the rear of Princess Alice Hospital; on 11 Carew Road; in the road near 35 Hartfield Road; in front gardens of 16/18 Hartfield Road; on 14 Hartfield Road; at the rear of 18, 25 and 39/41 Enys Road; in the rear garden of 18 Arundel Road; in the railway station goods yard; on platforms 1 and 2 of the railway station; on 62 Grove Road; at the rear of Bessant's, Grove Road.

Other HE bombs fell at the rear of 8 Furness Road; at the rear of 8 Grange Gardens; on 7 Grange Road; at the rear of 22 Grange Road; in front of 28 Grassington Road; outside 22 Silverdale Road; on The Seven Gables, Compton Place Road; in the grounds of Compton Place (now Compton Park); behind Powell House of Eastbourne College; opposite 18 Goodwood Bank (Close), Coopers Hill, Willingdon; in the garden of Chalk Farm, Willingdon; in fields at the rear of Chalk Farm; near Babylon Down and on Royal

The bomb that fell at the front of 13 Upper Avenue made a direct hit on a tree just to the left of the entrance driveway, blasting away all the branches and turning it into a shredded trunk only a few feet tall. The tree survives to this day, having grown a second set of branches and only in winter is it possible to see just how short and stocky is the trunk.

Eastbourne Golf Course.

More than 2,000 2kg Thermite incendiaries fell in the Terminus Road, station, Upperton area and in the Seaside Road and Cavendish Place area, also in the Carlisle Road area and in the vicinity of Chalk Farm, Willingdon.

Six unexploded bombs were suspected at 21 Silverdale Road, 13 Hartfield Square and around the junction of Hartfield and St Anne's Roads. Two more bombs fell in the sea and it is probable they came in the same load as the incendiaries in

A bomb exploded in the front garden of 13 St Anne's Road.

the Seaside Road area where off-duty Canadian soldiers did sterling work tossing sandbags onto the incendiaries, thus nullifying most of their effect.

The roof of St Anne's Church was completely engulfed in flames which could be seen from most parts of the town and the fire brigade fought long and skilfully to contain the blaze which eventually gutted the building, later compelling its demolition.

**CARELESS
TALK
COSTS
LIVES**

Wartime
injunction
from the
Government

The dead were: Mrs Mary Taylor, Mrs WE Walker and Miss S Boucher, plus the eight Canadian RAMC men. Six people were injured. In the circumstances, the low casualty rate was a miracle in itself.

The significant facts of this raid are – it was a deliberate night raid; it was intense; target illuminating flares were used for the first time over the town to ensure accurate identification of target areas; Canadian troops were in dispersed billets throughout each of the areas hit.

A few weeks before this raid, James Donne, a local journalist then serving in the RAF, attended a dance at the Winter Garden and there, with numerous others, heard some loose talk of a proposed seaborne raid by Canadian troops on the coast of France planned for the near future. The Canadians involved were to be drawn from the 2nd Infantry Division, some of whom had been billeted in Eastbourne until May when they were withdrawn for intensive training, being replaced by the Canadian 3rd Infantry Division.

One week after the air raid, men of the Canadian 2nd Division, plus British Commandos and other units, embarked for the ill-fated Dieppe raid.

Officialdom has vehemently denied any intelligence leak to the enemy but the night raid on Eastbourne, its target areas and the date – exactly one week before embarkation – certainly provide food for thought.

Thursday, August 13, 1942, 05.50 hours. Four Focke-Wulf FW190 fighter-bombers crossed the coast near Cooden and turned westward. Two dropped their 500kg bombs at Pevensey and Pevensey Bay then turned for home while the remaining pair came on to Eastbourne, raking the town with cannon fire and dropping one bomb near a gasholder, holing it and igniting the gas. The second bomb fell in Roseveare Road. Two people were injured.

Wednesday, August 26, 1942, 08.53 hours. Two FW190s crossed the coast near the Redoubt. One dropped its 500kg bomb on Marlow Avenue, destroying several houses, and the other's bomb fell on the Eastbourne Corporation Electricity Generating Station.

Frank Moore was killed outright and Mrs Lucy Dann and Mrs Ruth Chatfield of Marlow Avenue died in hospital. Seven people were injured.

One of the fighter-bombers was brought down into a ditch beside Lottbridge Drove by a Canadian bren-gunner who fired a long, speculative burst at the attackers as they crossed his front from left to right. The pilot was dead and it was noted that there was a bullet hole in the cockpit canopy.

The chaos in Marlow Avenue after the raid.   **September 5, 1942.** An enemy aircraft dropped a container of propaganda pictures of the Dieppe debacle on the Luxor Cinema, another sign that the air raid on Eastbourne on August 11 had been directly related to the heralded Dieppe raid.

Wednesday, September 16, 1942, 11.52 hours. A pair of FW190s came in very low and made for the station. Only one carried a 500kg bomb which it dropped on Platform One. The bomb ricocheted into the passenger dock where it exploded. The two aircraft then fired on Whitley Road, Annington Road, Beach Road and Seaford Road on their way out.

Six railwaymen were killed: Thomas Stevens, D Southgate, William Boniface, Sidney Bradford, Frederick Standen and E Griffin. More than thirty people were injured.

CHAPTER EIGHT
Unwelcome Christmas Present

*'. . . a Dornier 217 emerged from low cloud and rain and
at low level dropped four bombs so close together that
they were believed to be linked by chains.'*

A DEVASTATING compound explosion in the main shopping centre killed eighteen in the run up to Christmas and injured forty six. But first there was another raid that had tragic consequences.

October 26, 1942, 13.00 hours. An enemy medium bomber, reputedly a Dornier Do217 but more likely a Junkers Ju88, crossed the town from west to

The ambulance waits while rescue workers search through the rubble.

east with guns firing and over the Churchdale Road area it dropped four 250kg HE medium capacity bombs. One scored a direct hit on 69/71 Willoughby Crescent; another hit Seaside at the junction with Southbourne Road; a third passed through five walls of the Arlington Arms, crossed Seaside and exploded in the Alexandra Arms opposite, destroying the latter pub and adjacent houses; and the fourth is reported variously as a direct hit on 398 Seaside or on the edge of the pavement outside 396 Seaside.

In Willoughby Crescent, Mr and Mrs William Ripley, their son David, aged fourteen, and Mrs Ethel Mary Boniface were killed. In their home at 461 Seaside (close to the Alexandra Arms), Mrs Beatrice Maude Sherwood and her children Joan, ten, and Keith, five, died. Samuel Marley, driver of a bus caught in the midst of the strike, was killed.

Fatally injured were: Mortimer Boniface of Pevensey, Charles Burgess of Hydney Street, Douglas M Gower, thirteen, Grayson Wynne Baker, Mrs Mary Grant, Mrs Rose F Gearing and Louise R Burtenshaw, fifteen. In addition, twenty two others were injured – a grim total, but worse was to follow.

A casualty detector unit was used for the first time after bombs hit shops in Terminus Road. Here rescuers follow 'silent routine' as microphones are used to listen for the sound of survivors.

Rescuers turn their heads skywards as they hear aircraft engines while they struggle to free people buried under the rubble of Marks and Spencer.

Friday, December 18, 1942, 12.00 hours. Even in time of war Christmas continued to hold all its old magic. The streets and shops were thronged (comparatively speaking) with shoppers when a medium bomber, reputedly a Dornier Do217, flying east to west (some claim he came in directly from the sea) emerged from low cloud and rain and, at extremely low level dropped four 500kg HE medium capacity bombs so close together that many people claimed they had been chained together to achieve a devastating compound explosion – for that is certainly what it became – though the likelihood is that the low altitude of the bomber gave the bombs virtually no time to deploy.

One scored a direct hit on 45 and 47 Terminus Road (now 139/141); one was direct on 49 Terminus Road (now part of 139); two scored direct hits on Marks and Spencer, 51/53 Terminus Road (now 133/137). The area of destruction reached deeply to the rear of all the above premises and included Terminus Road Post Office (*not* Langney Road Post Office as it is often mis-named – Langney Road begins with the JobCentre).

Great difficulty was experienced in extricating those buried under the mountains of debris. The Mutual Aid Scheme was brought into operation and a Casualty Detector Unit was employed for the first time in Eastbourne. Wonderful work was performed by local ARP personnel assisted by reinforcements from Bexhill and Hastings (three parties), Kent Mobile Reserve (two parties), Tunbridge Wells, Hove, Lewes and Hailsham.

Troops from the Canadian 1st Infantry Division also provided maximum assistance. They were the 2nd Light Anti-Aircraft Regiment, 2nd Field Regiment, Princess Patricia's Canadian Light Infantry plus 569 Army Troops,

RE, 16 Field Construction Company, RE and 185 Pioneer Group, RE.

Further help came from the ET School, RAF, and 21st (Eastbourne) Battalion, Sussex Home Guard.

Those killed were: Theobald Vinsen, Mr J Smith, Mrs Eva Nicholls, Michael Nicholls (nine months), Mrs Daisy Ruth Gurr, Miss Jessie Cockburn, Mrs Edith Anker, Mrs Emily Julia Randall, Miss Kate Louisa Willson, Mrs Emily Elizabeth Packham, Jean Turner (eleven), Mrs Marjorie Bowen, Mrs Florrie Selway, Mrs Ethel Hart, Miss Anna Bonner, Mrs Edith Scott, Mrs Beatrice Chambers and Mrs Elizabeth White.

There were thirty seven injured by the bombing and an additional nine casualties among the rescuers who fell victim to falling debris.

Tuesday, December 29, 1942, 14.56 hours. Fighter-bombers completed the year's work for the Luftwaffe when two Focke-Wulf FW190s cleared Beachy Head and the Downs then, with guns blazing, dived across the town and

Teams of rescue workers in the remains of a house in
Victoria Drive – bombed on December 29, 1941.

dropped two 500kg bombs, the first of which struck allotments near Gildredge Hospital (off Longland Road), bounced over Longland and Dillingburgh Roads, passed through 67 Victoria Drive and exploded in number 62 across the street. The total distance from first strike to explosion is estimated at some 300 yards. The second bomb fell in gardens at the rear of the Old Court House, Moat Croft Road.

Mrs Charlotte Dry was killed, Mrs Harriet Marchant died in hospital and thirty-six people were injured.

The old year was at its end but the New Year was to bring no welcome changes to the status quo.

Friday, January 15, 1943, 14.00 hours. The local warning system, the Cuckoo, had been knocked out by a storm and so there was no hint of the enemy until four Focke-Wulf FW190s made a landfall at Beachy Head and dived across the town from the west, firing their cannon and dropping one 500kg bomb each. Numbers 33 and 35 Green Street were hit as were 3 and 4 Wilmington Terrace. Another bomb fell in a passageway between the Imperial

Numbers 33 and 35 Green Street suffered fearful destruction when a 500kg bomb struck on January 15, 1943.

HELL FIRE CORNER

The bomb which fell in the cleared area formerly comprising Cross Street and Duke Street was the last straw for the ill-used Bourne Street/Langney Road area. Badly battered in earlier bombing raids, it had come to be known locally as Hell Fire Corner because of the many sticks of bombs which criss-crossed the district, and few people chose to linger there. Cross Street and Duke Street had largely disappeared when a 500kg bomb effectively ended their existence permanently on January 14,1943. One has only to stand at the Langney Road/Bourne Street junction and gaze at the blocks of flats, the enlarged school playground behind and between the Rose and Crown and Salvation Army Citadel to gain at least some small idea of how this area suffered though the whole picture is still too broad to take in completely.

Above, devastation at Hell Fire Corner.

Hotel, situated in Devonshire Place, and Hartington Place and the fourth hit the cleared area of Cross Street and Duke Street.

The most serious of these strikes was that at Wilmington Terrace where it took twenty four hours to extricate those people trapped beneath the debris. The courageous and strenuous efforts of the rescuers came to nought when it was found that everyone was dead.

One man caught on the street was struck by a machine-gun bullet and died later in hospital.

The death toll in this raid was: Mr F Gosden, Mrs Frances Crowhurst, Miss Louisa Crowhurst, Mr AJ Kelly, Joseph Rayner, Mrs Daisy Rayner, Lily Jackson, Mr J Steed, Mrs Matilda Hughes and Mrs Lily Arnold. Thirty-eight people were injured.

Saturday, January 23, 1943, 09.50 hours. Four Focke-Wulf FW190s, having dropped their bombs on the Eastern, Central and Western Avenues of Polegate, causing fatal casualties and demolishing several bungalows, ran for home and, on the way, raked Old Town, Eastbourne, with cannon fire. Nobody was hurt and there was some satisfaction when it was heard that the crew of a Bofors gun sited at Cow Gap claimed to have shot down one of the raiders into the sea. Later, wreckage and the body of a German airman were washed ashore to confirm their claim.

Sunday, February 7, 1943, 14.47 hours. Four more Focke-Wulf FW190s swept

Firemen search through the wreckage after the raid in which four FW190s bombed and machine-gunned the town on February 7, 1943, killing nineteen people and injuring seventy two.

Russell and Bromley and Brufords, jewellers, of Terminus Road, were destroyed by the February 7 raid.

low across the town at 14.47 hours. Each carried a 500kg bomb, one of which scored a direct hit on the Central Fire Station, Grove Road, killing six National Fire Service personnel. A second struck 126/130 Terminus Road (now 62, 64 and 66 since re-numbering); another passed through the upper rooms of houses in Lushington Road, crossed the street and hit number 20, virtually demolishing three houses and severely damaging three others; and the fourth bomb fell on 10 Hardwick Road.

Again East Sussex and Kent sent rescue squads to assist and a Casualty Detector Unit attended.

The dead were: Section Leader JW Bailey, Leading Fireman Frederick Mewett, Firewoman Pearl Chitty, Firemen John Hunter, Frederick Duke and Walter Goacher – all of the National Fire Service; Miss Emily Pringle, Miss Christine Pringle, Miss Anne Pringle (all of 20 Lushington Road), Miss Florence Norman, Mrs Ruth Cree, Miss Emily Taylerson, Miss Ellen Tydeman and Miss Evelyn Wilson.

In addition four soldiers were killed and seventy two people were injured.

Though from the outset of the war many fire appliances had been dispersed to scratch fire stations around the town for safety reasons, the Central

Fire Station was still the hub of operations but its loss was swiftly overcome and the professionalism of these brave men and women saw that fire cover continued unabated.

Tuesday, February 9, 1943, 08.19 hours. Two Dornier Do217s machine-gunned Meads, Old Town and Hampden Park on their way inland. Only superficial damage was inflicted and there were no casualties.

Sunday, March 7, 1943, 12.52 hours. An assortment of 15 Messerschmitt 109s and Focke-Wulf 190s approached low across the sea and climbed sharply to clear Beachy Head where two of the FWs bombed early, one bomb falling near the Radar Station and one in a ploughed field. The whole formation then dived across the town where the remaining bombs were dropped. The

A 250kg bomb dropped by a Me109 fighter-bomber destroyed 2, 4 and 6 New Upperton Road near its junction with Upperton Road on March 7, 1943.

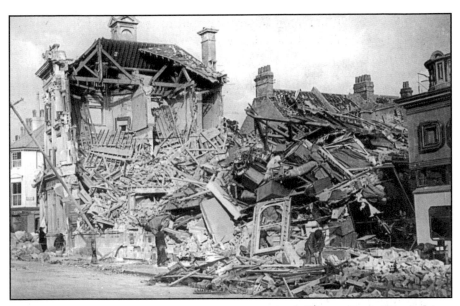

Barclays Bank and Prings, furnishers, took the full force of a 500kg bomb dropped by a Focke-Wulf fighter bomber on March 7, 1943.

MEs carried one 250kg bomb apiece and the FWs usually had one 500kg bomb each. One of the latter bombs struck the chimney of 3 and 4 Harts Cottages, Meads, broke up and also damaged numbers 2 and 5. A 250kg bomb bounced from Longland Road to Ocklynge Cemetery (a distance of about half a mile and something of a local record) where it killed two people. Numbers 2, 4, 6 New Upperton Road were destroyed, as was Barclays Bank in Terminus Road; 33, 35, 37 Cornfield Road; a Junction Road warehouse; 43, 45, 47 Jevington Gardens; Mostyn Hotel, Grand Parade; 22, 24, 26, 28 Meads Street; two 250kg bombs fell in rear gardens of 3 Staveley Road and 44 St John's Road.

Also recorded in the war damage index were: 29/31 Upperton Road and St Augustine's School, Milnthorpe Road. Two bombs fell in the sea between The Pier and Wish Tower.

For so many bombs to have been dropped by fifteen aircraft suggests that some of the FWs had been modified to carry two or more bombs. Later, the Air Ministry claimed that two of the attackers had been shot down.

Those who died were: William Payton, Mrs E Payton, Miss Annie Hollebon, Miss Alice Hollebon, Albert Newman, Donald Mackay, Mrs Ellen

Destruction at 6 and 8 Terminus Road on April 3, 1943.

The surface shelter in Spencer Road (near the junction with South Street) was of the simple 9-inch brick wall and 9-inch concrete roof variety intended only as a blast, splinter and debris shelter for people caught out of doors during an air raid. It was struck directly by a 250kg bomb which obliterated it and killed all inside.

Smith, Miss Violet Hipwell, Miss Henrietta Hollebon, Cecil Blake, Cornelius de la Roche, Miss Mary Perry, Miss A Currie and David Gilles. More than fifty people were injured.

Saturday, April 3, 1943, 11.45 hours. On this day ten assorted Me109s and FW190s dropped twelve bombs and inflicted the worst-ever casualty figures for a single raid on the town. It seems likely that either two of the FWs carried two bombs apiece or one (the FW190A-5/U3) carried two 250kg and one 500kg bomb.

The strikes were on: Park Gates Hotel in Compton Street; 2 and 4 Burlington Place; 6 and 8 Terminus Road (now 194 and 196); 2, 4, 6, 8,

The Park Gates Hotel, Compton Street, suffered severe damage during the April 3 raid by ten fighter bombers.

Ceylon Place; 105/113 Tideswell Road; 29/37 Longstone Road; 83/85 Avondale Road; gardens at rear of 278/280 Seaside; Sussex House, Harding Mews and Wish Cottage; a surface air raid shelter in Spencer Road; eight houses in Beltring/Firle Roads (astonishing damage for a reported single 250kg bomb).

One bomb passed through the Whitehall Hotel, Howard Square, and burst in the sea. The bomb on 6 and 8 Terminus Road, near Seaside Road, destroyed several shops and severely damaged Dale and Kerley's department store (now A & N) opposite. From the basement shelter under one of the smashed shops a number of people, some injured, were rescued while outside the fire brigade fought a blazing gas main.

Those who died were: Ethelbert Keay, WJ Edwards, Arthur Pidcock, Ernest Mason, FL Prodger, Miss L Brooks, Miss Mary Crisp, Peter Horton (twelve), Anthony Ellet (five), Joseph Hutchinson, Mrs Alice Dobell, Miss AK Oliver, Mrs Eleanor Cherryman, Mrs Grace Prior, Mrs Ethel Elson, Christopher Bonfiglioli, Mrs Dorothy Bonfiglioli, Miss Rose Lawrence, Mrs Ellen Williams, Miss Doris Hardwick, Betty Walker, Mrs Sarah Tidey, Mrs Edith McKinley, Miss Amy Bagshawe, Mrs EL Wilkins, Mrs Fanny

The remains of the Spencer Road air raid shelter after the raid on April 3.

Wren, Mrs FW van Mulbregt, Jacob Mulbregt, Mrs LG Thorne, Mrs Annie Colvin, GW Sargent, Petty Officer Davies RN and Mrs Kathleen Davies (the PO was home on leave but, being a serviceman, his death is not officially recorded in the town's list of local dead). Some ninety nine people were injured.

A young sailor, hearing the approaching fighter-bombers, snatched a baby from its pram and dived for cover, shielding the baby with his own body. The sailor died, the baby survived.

Once again the Air Ministry claimed that two of the attackers were hit.

Friday, June 4, 1943, 11.28 hours. A large number of aircraft, variously numbered as sixteen or eighteen, and reputedly all FW190s, approached Beachy Head at low altitude, climbed above the cliffs then dived across the town. ARP records of this raid have been lost but as fourteen bombs were dropped it seems most likely the number of fighter-bombers involved must have been fourteen; if there were more what became of their bombs?

The scene at the bottom of Grove Road when a 500kg bomb demolished several shops between Terminus Road and Ivy Terrace.

An accurate list of strikes is: Technical Institute/Central Library, Grove Road (now rebuilt as the new Central Library and Borough Treasurer's Department); MacFisheries, Grove Road (now Grosvenor Restaurant); garages at rear of 56 Woodgate Road; rear of 31 Bowood Avenue; 12, 14, 16, 18 Havelock Road; beside old Hospital Block, Ordnance Yard (in use as HQ of C Company, 21st [Eastbourne] Battalion, Sussex HG); in the roadway, Winter Road (now Winchcombe Road); 237 Southbourne Road; rear of 17/19 St Anthony's Avenue; Hotels Metropole and Glastonbury, Royal Parade (the former now rebuilt as Metropole Court flats; on the green near the Fishermen's Club, Royal Parade; an anti-aircraft gun site at Paradise Drive; junction of St Anne's Road and Commercial Road. A UXB passed through St Saviour's Vicarage and lodged in the church;

Those who died were: A Leitch, Mrs Cecily Ashdown, Mrs Emily Simmonds, Mrs Lily Hylands, Mrs Mary Walters, Mrs JE Harries, George Dorman, William Freeman. Thirty three were injured.

CHAPTER NINE
Unattached

'. . . one bomb approaching overhead with no Focke-Wulf attached!'

'I've got 'em! Six, ten, thirteen – no – fourteen of the blighters approaching me. South-east at zero 50 feet. Miles three. Now miles one. The first bunch approaching overhead. Fourteen Focke Wulfs approaching overhead with bombs attached. No, hold it. Correction. Thirteen Focke Wulfs approaching overhead with bombs attached. One bomb approaching overhead with no Focke Wulf attached!'

Record of report by a member of the ROC at 13.38 hours, June 6, 1943.

EXACTLY one year before D-Day, to the day, fourteen FW190s made the last severe attack of the war on Eastbourne. All bombs were of medium capacity and 500kg calibre – damage was consequently severe.

Sunday, June 6, 1943, 13.38 hours. Making landfall near Princes Park, the aircraft dropped bombs on the Crumbles (near the present Leisure Pool roundabout); Princes Park near Channel View Road; 35/45 Beach Road; open ground near the Gas Works; Caffyns Garage at the junction of Seaside and Seaside Road; 103/111 Ashford Road; 25/27 The Avenue; 27 St Anne's Road; 28/30 Lushington Road; 10 College Road; Beachlawn, Selwyn Road; 1 Pashley Road and Hildegarde, Meads Road. A bomb also passed through 13/15 Waterworks Road and demolished a cottage in the Waterworks yard;

Those killed were: William Cromwell, H Longworth, Harry Pinnington, Mr E Pinnington,

Caffyns' large garage in Seaside was destroyed.

72

Annie Child, Benjamin Hillidge, Mrs E Chapman and several military policemen. Forty three people were injured.

As they swung across Beachy Head on their way home some of the FWs fired on the Royal Observer Corps post on the Head where the ROC hut was peppered by cannon shells from the enemy – and bullets from would-be defenders firing machine guns from the radar station nearby.

The enemy was not quite finished with us but hereafter the raids on the town reverted to a more casual – and less lethal – nature.

July 30, 1943, 01.00 hours. Two 500kg bombs fell on the Crumbles near Pevensey Bay Road.

October 23, 1943, 00.26 hours. Two 250kg bombs fell on open ground near Langney.

November 7, 1943, 00.15 hours. One 500kg bomb fell on Babylon Down and another on Cornish Farm.

December 22, 1943, 22.30 hours. One HE fell in Brickfield Pond, Hampden Park. There was one slight casualty and slight damage to property.

December 30, 1943, 19.10 hours. One HE fell near Langney Priory; one landed behind Wholesale Meat Supplies' abattoir, Langney (now the junction of Faversham Road and Langney Rise) and a third fell on Bassett's Farm, Langney Rise (also listed as Batchelor's Farm). A UXB fell near Langney Fort Cottages, Pevensey Bay Road.

February 3, 1944, 22.45 hours. One HE landed on the foreshore near Wish Tower and a second fell in the sea just south west of the tower.

February 23, 1944, 22.05 hours. Five hundred 2kg incendiaries fell west of Beachy Head; one 50kg incendiary (UXB) landed near Hodcombe Farm; four 50kg incendiaries (two UXB) fell near Belle Tout – along with three HE; and one HE fell near Chalk Farm.

March 14, 1944, 00.55 hours. Three fighter-bombers made an uncharacteristic night raid. Crossing the coast near Langney Point with engines throttled back they dropped one HE bomb in the sea; one near 13 Hartfield Square (St Anne's Road), damaging property and setting military vehicles ablaze; one on tracks two and three at the railway station. Opening-up their engines they headed for home. Only one person was injured, and that was slight.

March 22, 1944, 00.40 hours. A twin-engined enemy aircraft crossed the coast from the south east and dropped one 250kg bomb at rear of 13 West Gardens and another on open ground at rear of West Crescent.

March 31, 1944, 03.35 hours. This was the last time manned enemy aircraft dropped bombs within the boundaries of the County Borough of Eastbourne. One 250kg HE fell on the Crumbles near Pevensey Bay Road; two 500kg HE fell near Willingdon Golf Course. Damage was slight.

There was no communal sigh of relief – audible or inaudible – at this event for no one in Britain could possibly know that an implacable enemy had at last given up on this form of warfare. Eyes and ears remained fully cocked for the expected drone of medium bombers, the snarl of fighter-bombers and the roar of cannon fire.

The Doodle-Bugs

Before the war there appeared on British speedway tracks midget racing cars bearing the American nickname Doodle-Bug and, when it was realised the sound of the V1's crude ram-jet engine was reminiscent of the sound of the midget cars, the weapon was also given the name Doodle-Bug. The cars are largely forgotten – the bombs are not!

British Intelligence had long known that Germany was preparing new weapons with which to attack us, and the Royal Observer Corps had been warned to look out for 'Pilotless Air Craft' as well as the conventional attackers. Six days after D-Day, at 4 am on the night of June 12-13, 1944, clear visibility enabled observers on Beachy Head to see, thirty miles away, the glowing tail of the first V1 flying bomb to be launched against England. It fell in open country, doing no harm. Later that day a confidential message was received stating: 'The enemy last night used P.A.C. (Pilotless Air Craft).' A few nights later there were a few more – a trickle which rapidly became a stream and later a flood which lasted ten weeks.

The V1s were designed to fly directly to London where their engines would cut out and they would immediately dive into the ground, causing the warhead to explode. Occasionally, London's barrage balloons would bring them down, but with exactly the same effect, and this also applied to the heavy anti-aircraft defences which had ringed the capital since the outbreak of war: the defences were no longer a protection against these early V-weapons.

To remedy this, the 3.7 and 4.5 inch anti-aircraft gun batteries were moved to the coast where they were set up to cover the numerous 'lanes' along which the V1s habitually flew. From that time on, when the first of a 'train' of V1s was sighted approaching the coast a rocket would be fired to indicate which lane and the big guns would open fire, the smoke of their bursting shells leaving long lines of black blobs tracing the course of the V1 until, suddenly, there would appear a massive dark cloud with a vivid red centre and the ram-jet engine would come cartwheeling out as the V1 died.

Fighter pilots returning from supporting the troops in Normandy also took a hand, shooting down quite a number of V1s but the real spectacular was to see pilots who, out of ammunition, would fly alongside the V1 and use their wingtips to gently tip the wingtip of the V1 until it was gradually turned to face back the way it had come, on which course its gyroscope would maintain it – a matter for grim satisfaction all round.

Although hundreds of flying bombs were destroyed in the air over or near the town, and many were turned back or shot down to explode on the ground in various parts of Sussex, it would be impractical to attempt to

The damage caused by a shot down V1 on June 18, 1944, was considerable. Several houses in Charleston, Milton and Mountney Roads were virtually destroyed, or had to be demolished for safety reasons.

record them here. The number that actually fell within the borough, however, was small considering the huge numbers despatched from France.

June 18, 1944, 20.25 hours. A V1 cut out and fell in the triangle formed by Charleston, Milton and Mountney Roads. Forty one people were injured and there was extensive damage to property – seven houses were destroyed and there was considerable blast damage.

June 20, 1944. A V1 fell alongside Butts Lane.

June 21, 1944. A V1 was shot down by fighters and exploded on the Downs.

June 22, 1944, 20.10 hours. A V1 fell at the Park Avenue entrance to Hampden Park, demolishing the tea chalet and damaging the Park Keeper's lodge. Three people were injured.

June 23, 1944, 22.45 hours. A V1 struck the cliff edge opposite the Beachy Head Hotel.

June 27, 1944, 00.35 hours. A V1 struck the cliff face near the lighthouse.

June 27, 1944. A V1 exploded in the air between Kings Drive and the Railway.

July 4, 1944, 19.00 hours. A V1 shot down by a fighter fell just behind Astaire Avenue houses. The fighter pilot, not apparently realising that a V1 fell instantly and vertically when hit,

A V1 shot down behind Astaire Avenue on July 4, 1944, caused tremendous blast damage to houses which later had to be demolished.

fired in expectation of it taking up a gliding angle and falling in open country – it did, by just a few yards. Thirty one people were injured, six houses had to be demolished and there was considerable damage to property over a wide area.

July 16, 1944, 24.00 hours. A V1 fell near Half Way Houses on the Downs.

July 27, 1944, 19.25 hours. A V1 fell on 68 Brassey Avenue, Hampden Park. Thirty six people were injured, six houses were demolished and many more badly damaged.

August 1, 1944, 15.36 hours. A V1 was shot down by fighters and exploded on the Downs.

August 1, 1944, 15.40 hours. A V1 exploded in the air over Old Town, the blast injuring three people and causing superficial damage to property.

August 3, 1944, 10.15 hours. A V1 was exploded by AA guns over Meads causing superficial damage to property.

August 6, 1944, 03.45 hours. A V1 fell near Beachy Head.

August 7, 1944, 23.16 hours. A V1, on fire, crossed the coast near Holywell and, because its motor kept running, lost height only gradually. It crashed and exploded near St Elisabeth's Church and Baldwin Avenue. Sixteen people were injured, several houses in Baldwin Avenue were demolished and there was severe damage over a wide area.

August 14, 1944. A V1 was destroyed over Meads by anti-aircraft fire; property was superficially damaged. This was the last recorded flying bomb that fell within the county borough.

On August 30 the main British/Canadian advance began from the Seine and within two weeks the whole of the 'Flying Bomb Coast' had been cleared – the threat was at last gone.

Withdrawal Symptoms?

THE battles in Europe had long since moved on to the German frontier when I came home on leave to find the cheerful and stoic Eastbournians at last showing signs of stress and war-weariness. People were less tolerant, more grumpy, there were fewer smiles and cheerful greetings. I could not understand it – after all, was the war not drawing to a successful conclusion, was the bombing not over?

Late one evening there came a familiar sound from the north east and many of us went outside to make sure our ears were not deceiving us. Sure enough, it was a Doodle-Bug, probably air-launched from a Heinkel 111 over the Thames Estuary and gone well astray. Fascinated, we watched the flaming exhaust pass across the town, over Beachy Head and out over the sea. A few minutes later the engine died and, after a pause, there was the familiar heavy thud of detonating TNT in the distance.

Morning came and, lo and behold, the smiles were back, the cheerful greetings had returned and the jokes flowed once more! I could not rationalise the change at first but soon came to realise that, to employ a modern term not then in use, Eastbournians had been suffering withdrawal symptoms!

George Humphrey

At last, anti-tank and anti-landing mines were cleared from part of the beach and children were able to play on the sand and in the sea again, after nearly five years. The scaffolding was put up to hinder the landing of vehicles.

Appendix 1
Raids, casualties and damage

RAIDS

High Explosive bombs which detonated on land...................................671
Unexploded bombs (eventual total)...90
Oil bombs which burst on land...28
Thermite incendiary and phosphorus incendiary bombs.............. ......4000 +
V1 Flying bombs exploded on or over land...15
Naval shells exploded on land...1
Machine gun and cannon fire attacks......................................20
Mines washed ashore (13 German, 5 British, 3 unidentified)..................21
Air raid warnings: General...1350
                Local (Cuckoo warnings)..861
Incidents.................. 112

CASUALTIES

	Civilian	Service
Killed or died of wounds	172	28
Severely injured	443	63
Slightly injured	489	92
Missing	2	0
Total	1106	183

(Note: Civilian includes public plus the police, fire brigade, ARP etc; Service comprises army, navy and air force personnel.)

DAMAGE TO PROPERTY

Houses destroyed...475 plus
Houses seriously damaged..1000 plus
Houses slightly damaged...10000 plus

ENEMY AIRCRAFT SHOT DOWN OR CRASH LANDED

August 16, 1940........................Me 110..Meads
September 9, 1940...................Me 109..Langney
May 20, 1942...........................Me.109..................Near top of Beachy Head
August 26, 1942.......................FW 190............................Lottbridge Drove
November 9, 1943....................Me.410.....................................Friday Street

Appendix 2
Bomb strikes on Eastbourne

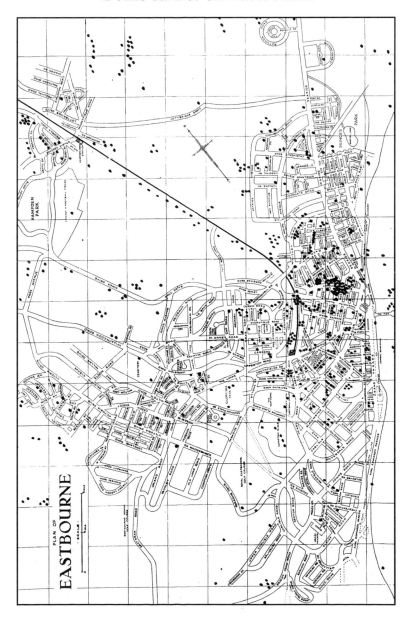

Appendix 3
V1 strikes on Sussex

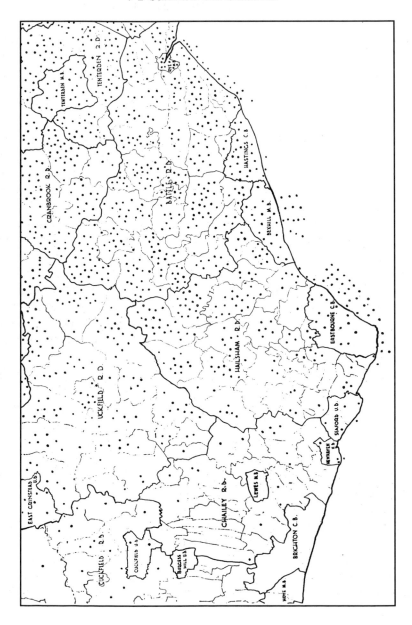

Appendix 4

Enemy bombers and fighter bombers

MUCH has been written and spoken about the capabilities of the Luftwaffe bombers. In general they were not as accurate as legend would have us believe and only the Junkers Ju87 dive bomber could truly be called accurate and, alas for the Germans, it was fatally vulnerable to Spitfires and Hurricanes with the result it was withdrawn from the Battle of Britain.

The main bomber to be employed against Eastbourne was the Dornier Do17Z-2 with some support from Junkers Ju88A-4 bombers and occasional night attacks by Heinkel 111 bombers. For some time after the fall of France, the Luftwaffe operated from forward grass airstrips which meant their bombers could take off only with their normal ground support bomb loads.

DORNIER Do17Z-2: This maid of all work was powered by two 1,000hp Bramo radial engines which gave it a loaded cruising speed of only 186mph. Its tactical range was very limited and its best ceiling was 13,000ft. Nor was its service bomb load of great consequence, being only 1,000kg (2,205lb) – about the same as a British light bomber – generally carried internally as one of two types of load. These were two 250kg HE bombs and eight 50kg HE bombs (approx 800kg) or three 250kg HE bombs and one 50kg oil incendiary (approx 800kg). For defence, the Do17 was armed with six machine guns.

JUNKERS JU88A-4: This versatile aircraft not only served in the bombing role but, later, also as a very effective night fighter. However, it is in the bomber role that it visited Eastbourne from time to time. Powered by two Junkers Jumo engines, each delivering 1,340hp, it was fast (a later development with 1,775hp engines reached approx 300mph maximum). The bomb load of 4,400lb was pretty much on a par with British medium bombers and its operational range was 1,110 miles. Whenever a Ju88 visited Eastbourne it generally carried four bombs of 500kg calibre.

HEINKEL He111: For a long time Germany's main heavy bomber, the Heinkel suffered badly during the Battle of Britain but came into its own as a night bomber. It bombed Eastbourne only during the night and when on its way to or from London or some other distant target. With a range of 1,275 miles at 240mph at 16,000ft and a bomb load of only 2,500kg (5,500lb) the

He111 was not really in the same class as the British heavies.

DORNIER Do217: Really an upgraded Do17, the 217 was powered by two 1,270hp Daimler-Benz engines giving a speed of 250mph and a range of 1,500 miles. It had a maximum load of 8,800lb of bombs, of which 5,500lb were carried internally. Again, when deployed against Eastbourne, this aircraft generally carried four 500kg bombs only although there is some evidence of sticks of jettisoned bombs numbering five.

In comparison with German bombers, the British Avro Lancaster could carry 22,000lb of bombs, depending on targeting requirements.

Both of the Luftwaffe's main fighters – the Messerschmitt Me109 and the Focke-Wulf FW190 – were also developed into fighter bombers, each maintaining its fighter armament while adding one or more medium capacity high explosive bombs of 250kg or 500kg calibre. Since the whole aircraft was virtually aimed at the intended target, a direct hit was far more likely with that one bomb than could be achieved by the medium bombers with a full load, and the damage and casualties they caused seemed out of all proportion to the actual weight of bombs. They came in fast, low and (usually) unheralded so that the residents' attuned hearing was more reliable than any formal warning.

MESSERSCHMITT Bf109 (Me109): Powered by one Daimler-Benz DB601A 12 cylinder engine developing 1,000hp or more, the 109 could fly at 336 mph in 1940 but this was increased to 400mph later. Armed with two 20mm cannon and two 7.9mm machine guns, it was a very effective fighter. In the fighter bomber role it could also carry one 250kg (550lb) high explosive bomb.

FOCKE-WULF Bf190 (FW190): This superb fighter originally had a BMW engine which was a development of the American Pratt and Witney Hornet radial engine (much improved) giving something like 2,000hp and a speed of around 400mph. As a fighter bomber, the FW190 could carry a maximum load of 1,000kg (2,200lb) as one, two or even three high explosive medium capacity bombs – one 500kg or one 1,000kg; two 500kg; two 250kg and one 500kg – according to target and requirements. In addition it carried four 20mm cannon and two 7.9mm machine guns.

Appendix 5

They also served

FORMED on May 14, 1940, the **21st (Eastbourne) Battalion, Sussex Home Guard**, began life as G Company, Sussex Local Defence Volunteers (LDV) and was at first commanded by Brigadier General EW Costello VC, CMG, CVO, DSO. Within a month or so, the LDV became the Home Guard, the Eastbourne unit was re-designated a battalion and comprised four companies, its total strength then being around 2,000 men – all armed with service calibre weapons despite legends to the contrary.

Command was later transferred to Lt Colonel Wise DSO, and later still to Brigadier General Charles Terrott DSO, who continued to command the battalion until June 1943 when Lt Colonel T Sutton MBE took over. During that year the battalion was increased to include some of the surrounding districts when B Company of the 20th Battalion was transferred.

In all some 5,000 men were reported to have passed through the ranks of the Eastbourne battalion at one time or another. There were more than thirty Home Guard battalions in Sussex alone.

The initial task at the inception of the LDV was one of watching for enemy paratroopers and the orders were to 'observe, report and harass' any incursions. However, as the risk of invasion increased, it soon became clear that the Eastbourne Home Guard would more likely be called upon to defend the town if the enemy should outflank it. Then, when the invasion threat

Lieutenant Freddie Morris, centre, and men of 10 Platoon C Company, 21st (Eastbourne) Battalion, Sussex Home Guard.

One of the four Browning medium machine guns of the Machinegun Platoon of the Eastbourne battalion, Home Guard, in the 'sustained fire' role at a public demonstration on Eastbourne seafront, May, 1943.

Every platoon of the Eastbourne HG had a Northover Projector weapon firing self-igniting 'Molotov Cocktails', anti-tank grenades or hand grenades. Here they fire Molotovs during the May 1943 display.

Men of Eastbourne Home Guard with 'Discharger-cup (E/Y) rifles firing hand grenades during the demonstration in May 1943. These weapons could also fire anti-tank and smoke grenades.

decreased the battalion continued to observe and to stand by lest a seaborne raid was attempted. In addition, assistance was given at many air raid incidents. Most men did two guard nights a week as well as attending Sunday training sessions – and all this on top of a normal working week. They never faltered, they never offered idle boasts, they were staunch, loyal and unbelievably effective soldiers.

The courageous work of the **ARP (Air Raid Precautions) wardens, first aid parties and rescue workers, of the fire brigade and the police** cannot be praised highly enough. Their devotion to duty, speed, efficiency and skill were of the highest order and, when infinite patience and compassion were required when working in the most treacherous conditions, they produced those, too.

The medical services – **doctors, nurses, the Red Cross and St John Ambulance Brigade** were also unstinting in their efforts to help the injured, and the townspeople played their part by gladly donating blood to the local hospitals.

Despite damage to its tracks, rolling stock and buildings, the **Southern**

Railway Company and its employees provided a remarkable service to and from the town with only minimal disruptions to timetables. A railway is a legitimate target for bombers, but nobody flinched from duty.

Another legitimate target was **Eastbourne Gas Company**'s works beside Lottbridge Drove, and the gasholders there were hit a number of times. Scarcely a raid occurred in the town without a gas main being fractured – and the consequent risk of fire. Time after time the company's engineers were called out, at all times of the night and day, to deal with the hazard of escaping gas, and restore the service.

Eastbourne Corporation Electricity Department also suffered damage to its mains and, to some extent, its buildings, but in general managed to keep the generators running and, at a time of smaller demand from the town, to feed power into the national grid to help the rest of the country.

The oldest publicly-owned bus undertaking in the world, **Eastbourne Corporation Motor Omnibus Department** (the initials are immortalised in Ecmod Road), suffered severe damage to its buildings and vehicles. Eight of its buses were requisitioned by government agencies, fifteen double deckers were hired out to an operator in Lancashire, and the company also provided transport for workers on defence projects after Dunkirk, and was on standby to move buses inland to provide transport for army reserves in the event of invasion. **Southdown Motor Services** also suffered losses and damage during the war and offered similar services to the authorities.

Before the war **Eastbourne Waterworks Company** took steps to ensure the continuity of supply in the event of air attacks on the town, recruiting local plumbers as auxiliary turncocks in case of emergency.

The town was divided into areas about half a mile wide and each area was provided with a standpipe so that every house in the town was within 500 yards of pure water in the event of a complete breakdown of mains supplies. All hospitals were supplied with their own storage tanks.

Thanks to the skill and efficiency of the company staff, there was seldom any major disruption of supplies, no matter the extent of damage to the mains supplies.

Little has been written of the **Royal Observer Corps**, a band of volunteers

The Eastbourne detachment of the Royal Observer Corps.

formed before the war to be trained in detecting and reporting enemy aircraft approaching Britain. These were the unsung heroes of the war in Eastbourne. These men had no uniforms until the third year of the war and even then had to part with valuable clothing coupons before receiving them. They stuck to their posts through all weathers, using eyes and ears to supplement the radar station's efforts and, often enough, being the first to report the approach of enemy aircraft, especially when they came in under the radar at sea level.

So great is the publicity given to radar (*r*adio *d*etection *a*nd *r*anging) that its shortcomings are often overlooked with the result that the work of the ROC tends to be played down. The observers manned lookout posts which, of necessity, were placed in the most exposed positions to ensure a clear view all round, and were completely uncovered. A ring of sandbags offered some horizontal protection but no overhead cover.

While the people of Eastbourne endured unheralded bombing raids because of the unbelievable edicts of Whitehall, the observers, the town council and the local press fought tooth and claw to have a local warning system approved and installed. When this desirable state of affairs finally became reality, it was still necessary to clear the warning with the area controller thirty miles away, with the result that the raiders arrived before the sirens could sound. The observers took matters into their own hands and gave the town a half a minute warning before the bombs were dropped. It was not a very long period of notice but, in the prevailing circumstances, was more than enough for the townsfolk to take cover.

On the second occasion the observers took this step the attackers passed over the town but did not bomb, and the observers received a severe reprimand – but they did not give up. So, on the principal that 'if you can't beat 'em, join 'em', Whitehall allowed the observers to use their own judgement. Even so, it was often a matter of a few seconds only before the enemy arrived.

Radar had one notorious weakness; it was virtually impossible to detect low flying aircraft and when the fighter bomber era began it fell to the ROC to spot the approaching aircraft against the gleam of sun off the sea, mist, rain, poor light. Often, as with most people at the time, they identified the aircraft as enemy by sound alone. The lives of the populace lay in the hands of these men with dedication, keen eyes and ears and quick reactions.

Initially commanded by Chief Observer JEF May, in 1941 the Eastbourne unit of the ROC came under the command of Chief Observer CB Lawrence.

Throughout the worst of Eastbourne's ordeal, two men in particular stood out above all others. They were not military men, firemen, rescuers, first aiders, wardens or from any of the numerous organisations upon whom we relied. They were **Arthur Edward Rush and Francis H Busby.**

Councillor (later Alderman) Rush was an Independent member of Eastbourne County Borough Council, and a leading businessman when, in November 1938, he was elected mayor. He served the usual one year until November, 1939, by which time the war had broken out. His fellow councillors then re-elected him for another term and, unwittingly, gave to the town the right man for the job of carrying us through the dark years. When bombs fell, Arthur Rush was on the scene, never interfering, always on hand to smooth over difficulties, console the injured or bereaved and 'get things done'. Whatever he did was done in a quiet, unassuming manner. He persuaded, never ordered, and when the need for a local air raid warning system was seen to be vital, it was he who led the battle with Whitehall to obtain the system. He worked hard at his job, never stinting, and he was never heard to complain of his lot. He had been given a task, and he did it brilliantly.

When Arthur was re-elected to the mayoralty in 1941 and 1942, local people recalled that after the Great War Alderman Harding, who served the town as mayor throughout the period of hostilities, had been knighted for his services and it was an almost universal hope that Arthur Rush would also serve out the war and receive such a well-merited decoration.

Alas, the complement of the council had changed and the attitudes of councillors with it. Despite much lobbying by the public and local papers, particularly by *Eastbourne Gazette and Herald* editor Thomas Palmer, who fought a wonderful campaign in an effort to persuade the councillors to re-elect Arthur Rush to office, too many had already made up their minds and, pointing out that the mayoralty was only within the 'gift' of the council, promptly appointed Alderman Miss Alice Hudson to succeed Councillor Rush. The townspeople were deeply offended by this act, however legal, and their hopes of seeing Arthur Rush suitably rewarded were dashed. Their anger was ice cold and their memories long.

A council workman has handed to Town Clerk, Frank Busby (right), a photograph of Winston Churchill, found undamaged in the wreckage of a house in Lushington Road after a raid in 1943.

Francis H Busby was a West Country man by birth, a solicitor by training and town clerk of Eastbourne. Another quiet man, Frank Busby was also one who 'got things done' and who served the council and townspeople to the very best of his ability. With Arthur Rush he was one of the mainstays of the town, also being ever present whenever bombs fell, and making the combination of mayor and town clerk a really effective force for good in the town. He was Arthur Rush's right hand, his 'chief of staff'. For the benefit of the town and its people, the combination of Arthur Rush and Frank Busby was as close to perfect as makes no real matter.

'. . . *most precious of all, my outstanding memories are of the warm-hearted kindness of so many of our Eastbourne citizens during the terrible days of strain and suffering through which our town passed.*' Arthur Rush

Appendix 6

Roll of Honour

Anker, Mrs Edith M
Arnold, Mrs Lily
Ashdown, Mrs Cecily Amy
Bailey, J W
Bagshawe, Miss Amy
Baker, Grayson Wynne
Baker, Mrs Mary Ann
Bates, Francis
Benjamin, Claude R
Blake, Cecil W
Bonfiglioli, Christopher
Bonfiglioli, Mrs Dorothy
Boniface, Mrs Ethel May
Boniface, Mortimer
Boniface, William
Bonner, Miss Anna
Bontoft, John Harrison
Boucher, Miss S
Bowen, Mrs Marjorie F
Bradford, Sydney
Britain, Henry Edward
Brook, Miss Mary
Burgess, Charles
Burtenshaw, Louise R
Chambers, Mrs Beatrice
Chapman, Mrs E
Chapman, Wilfrid John
Chatfield, Mrs Ruth
Chennell, Eric
Cherryman, Mrs Eleanor
Child, Miss Annie
Chitty, Pearl May
Cockburn, Mrs Jessie M
Collier, Alfred
Colvin, Mrs Annie
Cooper, Mrs A M
Cree, Mrs Ruth
Crisp, Mrs Mary A
Cromwell, William A

Crowhurst, Mrs Frances
Crowhurst, Miss Luisa E
Currie, Miss Auguston,
Dann, Mrs Lucy
Davies, Mrs Kathleen
De la Roche, Cornelius
Dobell, Mrs Alice K
Dorman, George O
Dry, Mrs Charlotte E
Duke, Frederick Roy
Edmonds, W J
Edwards, Frank Bertram
Ellett, Anthony
Elson, Mrs Ethel
Fly, Brian
Freeman, William
Gearing, Mrs Rose F
Giles, Mrs Olive G
Giles, Stanley Arthur
Gillies, David
Glen, William H
Goacher, Walter H
Gosden, F
Gower, Douglas
Graham, Mrs M A
Grant, F M
Grant Mrs Mary P
Griffin, John E
Gurr, Mrs Daisy Ruth
Gurr Thomas H
Guy, Mrs A
Hall, Lucy
Hardwick, Miss Doris K
Harland, Peggy
Harries, Mrs J E
Hart, Mrs Ethel L
Henman, Samuel
Hillidge, Benjamin
Hipgrave, Miss I
Hollebon, Miss Alice

Hollebon, Miss Annie
Hollebon, Miss Henrietta
Horton, Peter
Hudson, Mrs Laura O
Hughes, Mrs Matilda
Hunter, John Edward
Hurd, Frank
Hutchinson, Joseph
Hutchinson, Sydney A
Hylands, Mrs Lily N
Jackson, Lily
Jensen, Hans
Jones, Miss Ann L
Keay, Ethelbert Norman
Kelly, A J
Langford, Charles J
Lawrence, Miss Rose
Lawry, Miss Carol W
Leitch, A
Longworth, H L
Mackay, Donald G
McKinley, Mrs Edith
Marchant, Mrs Harriet
Marley, Samuel
Mason, Ernest E
Matthews, Mrs Winifred
Mewett, Frederick George
Moore, Frank
Newman, Albert Edward
Nicholls, Mrs Eva F
Nicholls, Michael
Norman, Miss Florence
Oliver, Miss A K
Owens, Dennis John
Packham, Mrs Emily E
Payne, J
Payton, Mrs E
Payton, William J
Penfold, Mary Adeline

Perry, Miss Margaret
Perry, Miss Mary
Pidcock, Arthur
Pinnington, Harry
Pinnington, Mrs E
Pringle, Miss Anne E
Pringle, Miss Christine J
Pringle, Miss Emily G
Prior, Mrs Grace E
Prodger, Miss F L
Randall, Mrs Emily Julia
Rayner, Mrs Daisy M
Rayner, Joseph
Rich, Charles
Richardson, Mrs Mary
Ripley, David Ronald
Ripley, Mrs Mabel
Ripley, Moses
Ripley, William
Sargent, George O

Sayers, Rose
Scott, Mrs Edith
Selway, Mrs Florrie
Myra
Shadbolt, Harry
Sherwood, Mrs Beatrice
Sherwood, Joan
Sherwood, Keith Arthur
Simmonds, Mrs Emily L
Smith, Mrs Ellen
Smith J P
Southgate, D R Y
Standen, Frederick
Steed, J
Stevens, John
Sevens, Thomas E
Strong, Mrs Lottie M
Taylor, Mrs Mary Moira
Taylerson, Miss Emily
Thorne, G

Thorne, Mrs L G
Tidey, Mrs Sarah
Turner, Jean
Turner, William Thomas
Tydeman, Miss Ellen J
Van Mulbregt, Jacobus
Van Mulbregt, Mrs F W
Vigor, Jane Emily
Vinsen, Theobald
Walker, Betty
Walker, Mrs W E
Walters, Mrs Mary Ann
White, Mrs Eliza
Wilkins, Mrs E L
Wilkinson, Mrs Myrtle
Williams, Miss Kate L
Wilson, Miss Evelyn M
Wise, Mrs Henrietta
Woolliams, Robert
Wren, Mrs Fanny

Appendix 7

Leading ARP/Civil Defence officials

ARP Controller: W H Smith (Chief Constable), retired April 1, 1943, succeeded by F H Busby, Town Clerk.

Deputy ARP Controllers: J A Fairclough and Inspector R S Crighton.

Chief Warden: Brigadier W E Costello. Succeeded in November 1939 by Sir George Lambert.

Deputy Chief Warden: Sir Robert Dodd.

Chief Assistant: Police Sergeant John Bull.

ARP Officer: Major G H Christie. Succeeded on August 1, 1940, by Inspector R S Crighton.

Assistant ARP Officer: H J Wood.

National Fire Service (formerly Eastbourne Fire Brigade and Auxiliary Fire Service): Chief Officer S A Phillips.

Police: Superintendent Archer (from April 1, 1943),

Senior Control Room Duty Officer: H J Wood, succeeded on January 1, 1944, by A J Page.

Responsible for Rescue Services: R Williams (Borough Surveyor).

Rescue Services Staff Officer: R V Harvey.

Casualty, First Aid and Hospital Services: Dr J Fenton (Medical Officer of Health).

Staff Officer to MOH: H T Hounsom.

Assistant Staff Officer (Training): A J Burnage.

First Aid Commandant: Dr R M Barron.

Senior Gas Identification Officer: L P Blackwell.

Billeting Officer: R Ticehurst.

Right, destruction of the Central Library on June 4, 1943, when an estimated eighteen enemy aircraft raided Eastbourne.

ABOUT THE AUTHOR

George Humphrey was born in Eastbourne on December 31, 1922, the son of George and Jessie Humphrey. He attended Christ Church Infants and Junior Schools, and Willowfield Central School. In 1937 he became an apprentice compositor for T R Beckett, proprietor of the *Eastbourne Gazette* and *Herald*. George joined the Air Defence Cadet Corps (forerunner of the Air Training Corps) in 1938 and in May 1940 left to join the LDV/Home Guard in which he served – reaching the rank of platoon sergeant – until entering the Royal Air Force in September 1942. He became an armourer first with Bomber Command and, later, with Coastal Command. After the war George returned to Beckett's as a proof-reader and soon afterwards began his researches into the war years in Eastbourne. George took early retirement in 1986. He has had nineteen crime and adventure novels published and one other book on Eastbourne's wartime ordeal. His greatest source of pride is in having served in 21st (Eastbourne) Battalion, Sussex Home Guard alongside men who had already proved themselves in battle to be some of the finest soldiers this country has ever produced.